6/4/2003

To John Frankel

Have fun Solving
problems & creating
Value

The
RUNT PIG
PRINCIPLE

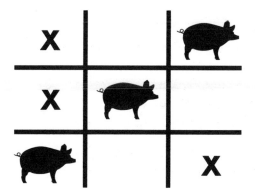

A Fundamental Approach to
Solving Problems
and Creating Value

CLIFFORD D. COOPER

For information, please contact:
Alliance For Progress Publishers
P. O. Box 5581
Balboa Island, California 92662
(714) 675-8438 Phone
(714) 673-3113 Fax

Library of Congress Catalog Card Number: 92-81924

ISBN #:0-9633046-0-7

Printed in the United States of America

To Louisa for all her loving support.

To our children, four and four:
Cindy, Corky, Dennis, George,
Jim, Liz, Marti, and Rick

To their spouses:
Cookie, Laurie, Mark,
Phil, Ray and Tom

To the memory of my friend Leroy Aven.

Contents

Section Four — The Leaders

Section Five — Taking Off

"The Principles"

Acknowledgments

Louisa and I were in Montreal, Canada, attending a Chief Executive Organization education forum, having dinner with our friends Henry and Ruth Blackstone. Henry and I started reminiscing about our many enjoyable past associations. I began telling them about some of my early life experiences. Henry listened to several of my stories and then said, "Clifford, you should write a book about your life. My daughter Margaret, who works for E.P. Dutton in New York, could be helpful."

I called Margaret after returning home and had a most constructive conversation. A few days later I received an encouraging letter as well as some basic advice on writing and publishing. The letter was signed "Meg Blackstone (Henry's kid!)." I am grateful to Henry and "his kid" for getting me started — it seems that *getting started* is most difficult.

Jodie Belknap, of Belknap Publishers in Honolulu, was very helpful during my extended stays in Hawaii. Jodie's advice on publishing and her efforts in putting some of my original writings on a computer were appreciated. Annie Fanning, a talented young student writer from Honolulu, and Kirk Wolcott, a student at UCI, helped during my early writing effort.

Alice Remer assisted me with her excellent editing skills during the final phase of preparing the manuscript. It was a pleasure working with Alice, and I appreciate her sincere creative contribution. Eula Palmer of Baypointe Services provided overall direction in preparing the book for publication. Her professional project management and desktop publishing skills added creativity and quality to the production process.

My artistic wife Louisa served as my best constant critic and adviser from the beginning to the end and made a major contribution to the design of the cover.

Many of my good friends have read the stories from time to time and offered constructive suggestions. J. R. Brown, an old friend from the Texas Panhandle, assisted in helping collect photographs. My friend Glen Muncy from Kansas sent me some prize photographs and suggested a change in the Eisenhower story. Orin Harvey, a lifelong friend and business associate who played a part in my success at Lights, Inc. and then at CDC, made some helpful suggestions. Thanks also go to Ray Pollock, Austin "Tex" McLaughlin, Robert D. Ladd, and Paul Bennet for their thoughtful contributions.

Prologue

A few years ago, I was invited to give a series of talks to the graduating class of the business school of the University of Southern California. After each talk, the students would gather around to ask questions. The most common question was "How do I get started?" This basic question caused me to look back at my life experiences in an attempt to find an answer. I began an examination and analysis of my activities in the early years when I first found the need to earn a living. This exercise revealed to me not only how I got started, but also a consistent pattern in my approach to problems, which I was not aware of at the time.

This pattern, I'm convinced, can work as a guide to any problem-solving situation. I call it "The Runt Pig Principle."

Section One
GROWING UP

*"How beautiful is youth, how bright it gleams
with its illusions, aspirations, dreams."*

— Longfellow

*"Fortunately for us and our world,
youth is not easily discouraged."*

*— General Eisenhower
May 27, 1946*

1.
The Runt Pig Principle

I was raised in Hart, a small farm and ranch town on the high plains of the Texas Panhandle. It is said that from the high plains you can look farther but see less than from any other place in the world. It was a land where the Great Depression met the Dust Bowl.

The dust blew in from the north and the west, blocking out the sun, turning day into murky twilight. Sometimes the dust made it impossible to drive a car or even to see across the room in our house. At night we hung wet sheets around our beds to collect the dust and keep it from settling on our bodies and sifting into our mouths.

Cyclones, blue northers, forked lightning, and hailstorms were the main topic of conversation in the Panhandle. Cyclones whirled across the flat land with funnels like claws, tearing apart everything in their paths. Sometimes the cyclones were so gigantic that they could be seen churning up the soil as far as fifty miles away. Hailstorms rained marble-sized stones, beating our meager crops to the ground. Often, some of the larger chunks of ice struck our cattle in the head, killing them instantly. Jagged lightning flashed across the sky day and night, accompanied by fearsome crackling sounds and cannon booms. Blue northers blew in with snow and tumbleweeds at velocities of up to seventy miles per hour, driving us into our dugout homes and cellars which we had built for protection against the blasts.

Harsh weather was a part of living on the high plains, and whenever possible, we used it to our advantage. All the farms and ranches had windmills that pumped water free of charge. The water fed our gardens, which in turn provided most of our daily food.

Each family grew extra crops for sale at the market. Farm production, while never abundant, was ample. We separated our milk and sold the cream each week to buy flour, sugar, salt, and other basic commodities. The hens laid eggs, and the fryers were sold for profit. We raised beef cattle to sell and for meat for the table. We skinned the cattle that we ate and sold the hides. Turkeys were sold for cash, except for those that the family consumed on Thanksgiving and Christmas.

We were self-reliant people. We had adequate food and shelter, but very little cash. Some years we would raise milo maize, a form of Indian corn. Wheat and cotton yielded additional income, but more often than not, the Dust Bowl conditions wiped out most of our crops.

Although my father was hardworking and essentially an optimistic man, the difficult farming conditions began to depress his spirits. To provide for our family of eight, he went away to work in the oilfields, leaving my mother at home in Hart to care for the children.

I was in my early teens when my father left home, and it became necessary for me to find a job. Most of the economic activity in the town centered around buying and selling cattle, hogs, horses, and mules. Roby Cregg, a neighbor of ours, ran one of the trading pens where cattle and hogs were bought and sold. I asked him for a job.

"I'm sorry, Clifford," Roby said, "but I just don't have any money to pay your wages."

Discouraged, I went home to talk to my mother who always encouraged my efforts. She explained to me that 'most everyone was suffering difficulties in these hard times, trying to find work. She said that she had great confidence in me, and that I should keep trying.

That evening I did some heavy thinking and came up with an idea. The next morning I went back to Roby Cregg and told him that I had a plan. I would work for him at his trading pens, but I wouldn't collect cash for my labor. Instead, he could pay me with runt pigs. As these little piglets were the smallest of the litter, they were considered worthless. Too tiny to compete with the larger off-spring for the sow's milk, they were usually killed by the mother or destroyed by the pig's owner.

Roby wanted to know what I expected to do with the runt pigs, so I told him my idea. He thought that my plan was a clever one. With his encouragement, I immediately set to work.

I began by removing the runt pigs to their own pen in the yard. Then I made a deal with Otto Denwitty, the owner of a four-room hotel and restaurant next to the local train station. I collected the unwanted slop and skim milk from his kitchen in ten-gallon cream cans and took them away for him each day. I made another deal with Homer Hill, who owned a large grain elevator. I cleaned the elevator for him, and in return, he let me keep the spilled grain swept from the floor. I took the grain, soaked it in the slop and skim milk and fed it daily to my runt pigs.

My tiny pigs began to grow. They grew up faster and became a little bigger than the normal-sized pigs in the litter. Mother Nature, it seemed, had given the runt pigs a stronger will to survive than their siblings. This resilience and the proper food and care I provided gave them an edge over the others.

It was not long before I began netting some income. My runt pigs had become well-fattened hogs that brought a healthy price at the market. Roby helped me sell my animals, and despite the troubled times, my efforts paid off. With the money I earned, I was able to help my family.

The Runt Pig Principle . . .

The greatest solutions, like the greatest joys in life, are often the simplest ones. Look around and see what is available to you. Use your strengths. Be willing and happy to work for what you want. When given the opportunity and proper encouragement, even the tiniest runt can grow into a strong, healthy, and valuable creature.

2.
Matching Mules

L eck Aven, my first adopted father, lived on a farm just north of Hart, Texas. When it came to trading cattle and horses, Leck was one of the best in the high plains territory. When it came to matching mules, Leck couldn't be beat.

I heard the story many times of how Leck brought his family from Arkansas to Texas in a covered wagon. Across the wide and barren plains they traveled, using the rutted cow-trails as their only guide. He traded and matched mules along the way to support his large family. After a long and exhausting journey, they finally arrived in the Panhandle of Texas where he took up dry land farming. A bright and able man, Leck had the skill and foresight to acquire two pairs of perfectly "matched" mules before the Great Depression.

After my father went to work in the oilfields, the rest of my family moved away from the Panhandle and I went to live with the Avens. They welcomed me into to their already large family of three boys and five girls. I helped out with chores around the house and worked in the fields during harvest season. Leck's second oldest son, Leroy, and I soon became great friends; he was like a brother to me. Our friendship was one of the most important influences in my life. Similarly, my relationship with Leck Aven was as constructive and satisfying as any between a natural father and son, and perhaps even better.

I was proud of Leck and I frequently went along with him when he visited one of the trading pens in town or took off on a trip around the countryside. I would sit and listen to the farmers and ranchers as they negotiated various deals. They would stand around at first, carefully looking over the animals that were being offered. Every so often, as the negotiations heated up, one of the traders would take out his pocket knife and start whittling on a stick, feigning indifference to the important trade that was going on. The trading process, I saw, was a matching of wits.

Leck loved to trade. He never missed a chance to bargain for a mule, and frequently purchased a single mule on a moment's notice. On such occasions we would load the animal into the two-wheeled trailer that Leck pulled behind his pickup truck. Day or night, and any season of the year, if the right mule was up for sale, Leck Aven was prepared to make a deal. Riding in the pickup with Leck gave me plenty of time to ask him how I, too, could become a smart mule trader.

"A pair of matched mules is always worth more than their combined value standing alone," Leck carefully explained. "The better the mules are matched, the more they are worth.

"When matching mules," he went on, "they should always be as close to each other in size as possible. This means the same height, the same weight, and the same general body formation. The mules should also be the same age and coloring.

"In the field," he added, "if a pair of mules is truly matched, they will know how to work together."

One day, Leck took me out to the barn to demonstrate exactly what he was talking about. He selected a pair of mules from the pen and harnessed them together. He pointed out the important matching characteristics — size, height, color, and body formation. Next, he opened the animals' mouths and examined their teeth to show me that they were the same age.

This was a perfectly matched pair of mules; they looked like twins.

Leck then drove the pair of mules out to the machinery yard and hitched them up to a large one-way plow. The plow was stuck deep in the ground and was very difficult to move. Both mules began pulling on their own, straining hard against the plow. The plow, however, stuck fast in the ground. It would not budge.

"Clifford," Leck said, "watch this."

Leck made an odd sort of clucking sound with his mouth and struck the mules lightly with a leather line. The mules began to move in a swaying motion to the clucking noise. First they moved backwards, then sideways, and finally forward. Moving together, as in a dance, they pulled the plow free and pranced across the field, dragging the plow easily behind them. As the mules raced down the field, Leck explained the value of cooperation and teamwork. "Combining individual talents," he said, "provides for an outstanding amount of achievement."

Although neither one of the mules could have moved the plow alone, together they had the power and strength of three or more animals.

"Remember this always," Leck said to me: "A perfectly matched pair of mules will know how to dance together."

Success and happiness depend upon how well you match with your friends, your spouse, and your business partners.

3.
The Five-Dollar Mule

R aising runt pigs at Roby Cregg's pens put me in contact with a number of cattle and horse traders. Most of these men worked on farms and ranches of their own and did their trading on the side. Some of the most successful farmers in the area were also the better traders.

Leck Aven, as I have mentioned, could trade with the best of them. His experience trading mules during his journey from Arkansas to Texas was practically a legend with the townspeople in Hart. Leck, an admirable man in numerous respects, was considered by many to be one of the smartest mule traders in the country. He recognized that value in mule trading is created through careful observation and astute matching.

As I considered myself a young man endowed with a fair degree of intelligence and a knack for careful observation, I was quite optimistic about my prospects in the mule trading business. What could be easier, I thought, than matching mules?

Armed with confidence and determination, I set out planning my career as a mule trader. The runt pig business had been a great experience for me and I envisioned sure success once again, prior to making my first mule deal.

Having sold a number of my fattened runt pigs at the market, I was ready to invest my profits. I decided to buy a mule and at once enter the ranks as a mule trader. I located a mule for sale about twelve miles west of town, contacted the mule's owner, and made a deal to buy the animal. My initial investment was five dollars.

After making the purchase, I went to the Aven's farm to tell Leck about my mule. He suggested that we drive out and take a look at my newly acquired animal. So, climbing into his old pickup — the trailer hooked to the back to cart home my prized possession — we drove out of town.

We arrived at the mule owner's farm in the early afternoon. Leck parked the pickup and we headed toward the pasture where my mule was kept. It was about a half mile walk from the farmhouse to the pasture. I became more and more excited with every step.

Leck and I reached the pasture. We climbed through a barbed wire fence and walked toward the animal. When we came within 400 yards of my mule, the beast suddenly bolted, running awkwardly away from us. Leck stopped in his tracks and took a good, long look at my mule as it lumbered across the grassy pasture. Then he turned and looked at me with a mixture of amusement and pity.

"Clifford," he said, "my advice to you is to have that old mule shot. Put the poor thing out of its misery. That is one sorry creature. I can see from here that it's badly afflicted with fistula and God only knows what else."

That afternoon, I was educated on rule number one in trading mules. It was a common sense rule that applies to business in general, and that is, always get your advice *before* making a deal, rather than after.

This was a very painful experience for me. Money was hard to come by at this time, and because of my own inexperience, I had foolishly thrown away hard-earned cash. However, in the years that followed, I came to see this episode in my life as an extremely valuable lesson.

Not only did I learn a great deal about business transactions that day, but I also discovered that I had no further interest in becoming a mule trader.

When expert advice is available to you, don't be too proud to ask for it and use it.

4.
Bird Cox and the Gas Station

U p the road, a half mile or so from Leck Aven's farm, Bird Cox owned a gas station. It was situated on the dusty dirt highway which ran from Plainview, passing through Hart on its way to Hereford. The year was 1933 and jobs were scarce.

I had known Bird most of my life. He was a rather short, heavyset man who was very likeable, but a bit on the lazy side. He was in his early forties at the time and married to a tall, robust woman named Bessie Mae. They had one child, a son named Claude, who had lost an eye in an accident when he was young.

Bird had been operating his gas station by himself for several years and offered the only gasoline service in the area. Farmers gathered at his place whenever they came to town. They stood around the big coal stove, warming their bones against the chill and windy winter, voicing opinions on the weather and exchanging information on the price of grain, cattle, hogs, and the like.

My whole family had left Hart for Del Rio, Texas, some three hundred miles to the south when I was seventeen. Now it was time for me to leave Leck Aven's family and be on my own. Bird needed help around the station and I needed money and a place to stay. When Bird offered me employment at $20 a month, room and board included, I jumped at it. I moved into the station, where I installed a small cot. I ate my meals with Bird and Bessie Mae in their house which was located in Hart within walking distance of the station. By working and sleeping on location, I could provide 24-hour gasoline service.

Frequently customers would come by the station after I had gone to sleep or early in the morning before daybreak and honk for service. I would get up and take care of their needs. This was hard work, especially during the cold, windy winters, but I kept reminding myself of my goals and objectives. I was working with the thought of saving my money to go to school. As a result of my mother's influence when I was a little boy, I had always wanted a college education and was further encouraged by Leck, Bird, and other friends to pursue this goal.

Soon after I began working with Bird, I saw potential in his run-down gas station and began visualizing ways to improve it. The station, a sagging old wooden shack, had only two pumps when I moved in. Bird sold a small amount of gasoline and oil to the farmers who gathered at his station, but little in the way of automotive and farm equipment supplies. He was content just to break even, and didn't go out of his way to provide extra services and products for his customers. Consequently, the farmers in Hart had to drive miles away to Plainview or Hereford to buy other needed products. They would have been only too pleased to buy these supplies from Bird, but he never took the initiative to put these items on his shelves.

Taking a look around the station, I realized that with a few simple changes, Bird's run-down gasoline stop could become a very profitable, full-service automotive and farm supply business.

I discussed my ideas with Bird and saw a receptive flicker of interest in his eyes. We got to work immediately. With our own hands, we rebuilt and enlarged the station to make room for tires, engine parts, and tools. I also walled off a small private sleeping area in the back for my cot. We built a lean-to warehouse onto the station and obtained some 55-gallon oil barrels to hold bulk oil and gasoline.

Because we were short on working capital, I located an automotive supply dealer in Plainview who would furnish us with reasonably priced merchandise on consignment. This allowed us to supply our customers with more of their automobile and farm equipment needs without putting up any of our own money. We also arranged to purchase oil and gas directly from the oilfield refineries. To finance these transactions we would obtain checks in advance of delivery from our customers by offering them a good discount. This enabled us to sell our products at a lower price while reaping a steady profit for ourselves. It didn't take long before we had turned a mediocre business into a thriving enterprise.

Imagination, initiative, energy, and determination are the keys to solving problems and creating value.

5.
Good-bye Dust Bowl

B ird Cox and I began to see the fruits of our efforts. The Cox Oil Company was increasing its customer base as well as its profits. To meet the demands of our many customers, we put our profits to work and bought a used Ford pickup.

The old pickup, however, had a mind of its own. It had a distracting tendency to break down about as often as it would start. My experience with cars up to this point was limited, but I found myself assuming the role of mechanic, as well as wholesaler and service man at the station. Attacking each problem, one at a time, I learned the ins and outs of the engine. I was soon able to rework the entire engine and could fix just about anything that ever went wrong with the truck. My knowledge came strictly from experience. For me, it was the best way to learn.

The gas station continued to prosper and I put away enough money to buy an old Ford coupe of my own. The mechanics I had learned keeping the pickup running enabled me to take apart the engine of my own car and rework it from front to back. After getting its innards in good working order, I turned my attention to its appearance. I painted it a bright yellow with a slick black racing trim. What a machine!

Leroy Aven, my best friend at the time, was a tall, slender man much like his father, Leck. Young as he was, he had a sharp, weathered face, and like his dad, a rather dry sense of humor.

Leroy could poke fun at anything or anyone, including himself. He didn't talk much, but when he did, he had something thoughtful and important to say. He had a remarkable memory and was an exceptionally good listener, a characteristic I deeply valued. He was always up front in his business dealings, took time to help people in need, and was trusted and respected by just about everyone.

With me behind the wheel and Leroy at my side, we tore up the countryside in my flashy yellow car with the slick black racing trim. Free and easy, we enjoyed the warm Texas summers. When we weren't busy working, we spent our days and nights in my car, courting the prettiest farm girls we could find.

I'd been working for Bird for about two and a half years, holding fast to the idea of going to college. Looking to the future, I had allowed Bird to invest my monthly wages back into the station for structural improvements. This helped him and became a savings for me, because he agreed that when the time came for me to leave for school, he would start paying me back the money I had invested with a check each month.

My preparation for college was not the best. The schools in Hart suffered a shortage of faculty, requiring the teachers to deal with several grades simultaneously. Most of the students, myself included, did not gain much of a formal education. Most of what I had learned came from work experience. I knew that I had to leave Hart to get the education I desired.

Jimmie Thomas, a local boy, had a friend in Ontario, California, who was attending Chaffee Junior College. He sent us some information on Chaffee and we discovered that the college offered a "6-4-4 plan" which would combine the last two years of high school with the first two years of college, and thus permit us to make up our high school deficiencies. The three of us, Jimmie Thomas, Leroy Aven, and I, who were all in the same boat academically, felt that this was tailor-made for us. We made arrangements to attend Chaffee.

I worked my Ford into good running condition for the trip west and made a slight alteration. I strapped a 30-gallon oil drum into the trunk for an extra supply of gasoline and connected it directly to the gas tank. I also stored two cases of oil in the trunk. With this added capacity, we could figure on getting most of the way to the coast without having to buy more fuel. Then I got together with Leroy and Jimmie to make plans for our adventure. We packed up our scant possessions, mapped out an itinerary on Route 66, and set a date for our departure.

On the day before our trip, Leroy's mother asked him not to go with us. She told him that it was his responsibility to stay on the farm and help earn a living for the family. This came as a tremendous disappointment for both of us. We had been planning the trip to California for some time and had become closer than blood brothers. Without a family of my own close by, I found it hard to leave behind someone who had come to mean so much to me. I could only look forward to the day the two of us would be together again. But for now, I was determined to go to college, and nothing was going to change my mind.

Bird was sorry to see me go. I was practically running his company by myself at that time and it worried him to be losing my services. However, he promised once again to send my wages to me once I was settled in California.

Jimmie and I left Texas before daybreak on a summer morning in 1936. As we set off on our journey, I was filled with a most powerful feeling of freedom and excitement. I had been reading Tennyson's *Locksley Hall* around that time and the poet's words came into my mind, perfectly suiting my mood:

Make me feel the wild pulsation that I felt before the strife,

When I hear my days before me, and the tumult of my life;

Yearning for the large excitement that the coming years would yield,

Eager-hearted as a boy when first he leaves his father's field...

Dreams fuel the world. Be bold in chasing your own.

Cooper brothers in the Texas Panhandle at the time of the
Depression and Dust Bowl: Cleo, Cliff and Fowler (left to right).

Amarillo Globe News Photo File

Tornado near Hereford
in the Texas Panhandle.

A Panhandle dust storm, April 14, 1935.

A farmer inspects his crop after a dust storm in the Texas Panhandle. Sand has drifted across the field destroying the crop and soil.

Section Two

OPEN ROADS

"Afoot and light-hearted I take to the open road,
Healthy, free, the world before me,
The long brown path before me leading wherever I
choose."

— Walt Whitman

6.
Route 66 in Quest of Education

J immie Thomas and I headed west toward California to go to college. As we drove along Highway 66 in my yellow Ford coupe, the treeless dusty plain that was the Texas Panhandle disappeared behind us. The Dust Bowl gave way to new and exciting territory. As the miles passed, our eyes were greeted with fresh and unfamiliar views. We explored side roads. Every road marker was an invitation to a new adventure. We ate and slept in the open air, savoring our freedom.

As I lay under the heavens, gazing at the stars, I thought about how I came to be in this place at this time, and about my goal of a college education. I realized that although I lacked book learning, I'd had certain advantages. While most homes in the Panhandle had only two books — the Bible and the Sears, Roebuck Catalogue — my home had my mother, Cordelia, who was well aware of the value of reading. She had a few books of poetry tucked away in the kitchen. She dipped into these, as well as into the flour, as she cooked the meals for our family. I would sit on a tall wooden stool and watch my mother prepare supper as she read poetry aloud or sang old ballads to me.

From the time I was a child, I can remember my mother talking to me about how important it was to have a college education. It was a dream of hers that I would some day go to California and study at one of the universities. She had always wanted to go to California herself, but the responsibility of six children and the poverty we suffered had prevented her from doing so. She had kept up a correspondence with some family members who had settled in California during the Gold Rush.

"Cliff, my son," she would say to me, "you go to California and get an education. Build a new and beautiful life, and enjoy yourself always. Through your eyes, I will see the beauty of California."

She gave me her books of poetry because she could see that I enjoyed them so much. Her gift showed me the vision of a better life and a world of beauty and possibilities beyond the Dust Bowl.

Even so, leaving Hart for the first time saddened me. This was, after all, the land where I had grown up. I didn't realize it at the time, but later I'd come to know that all my memories and the way I would look at the world in years to come were shaped during my boyhood in the Dust Bowl.

Now, as we made our way west to California, I was living not only my own dream, but my mother's as well. The sorrow I felt about leaving home was soon replaced by the excitement of my first journey. Jimmie and I stopped wherever we pleased, to admire the unfamiliar landscape. The jagged mountains and steep, towering buttes of New Mexico overwhelmed us with their changing color and grandeur.

As I traversed western America and took in all its beauty, I understood the yearning of the poets I had read. I recalled these lines from Walt Whitman's *Song of the Open Road:*

"To see no possession but you may possess it, enjoying all without labor or purchase, abstracting the feast yet not abstracting one particle of it..."

The Grand Canyon state of Arizona with its painted deserts and old mining towns was an even match for the wonders of New Mexico, but we found our excitement growing as we approached California, our destination. To go to school, to learn, to grow — these were the reasons we had traveled the long and open miles from Hart.

After crossing the Colorado River into California, everything began to look even more beautiful to me. My senses were heightened. The desert seemed more colorful, the mountains more majestic, the air more perfumed than before. The forests were deep and mysterious. The palm trees and the orange groves were truly exotic. We had come from a place that had its own stark beauty, but now we felt as though we were entering a paradise.

We were in no hurry. We took some side trips off the main highway and discovered paved roads, a novelty to us, and elegant homes partially hidden by orange groves in full blossom. With their sweet fragrance and dark green foliage, the orange trees were what impressed me the most and what I remember most fondly from my first journey into California.

We finally arrived in Ontario and located Chaffee Junior College. Jimmie's friend, a policeman, helped us get settled. We took an apartment on Euclid Avenue, four blocks south of the college. Our room provided a pleasant view, looking out across the avenue with its double rows of trees and shady green median. Rent came to six dollars a month each. For this sum, we had one room, the use of the bathroom, and an outside front porch where we could sleep on hot nights.

Jimmie and I enrolled at Chaffee and began attending classes. The dean of men, a math teacher, helped me adjust to college life. With my lack of formal education, I found school to be difficult. My reading ability was inadequate for this level of education and I struggled daily to catch up. I was able to earn "A's" in math and in any subject that did not require much reading. This did wonders for my confidence.

I had arranged with Bird Cox, before leaving for California, for him to send the money he owed me in monthly payments. The first month in my new home came and went without a word or a check from Bird. My finances were dwindling, but I was patient and waited.

A week or so passed when I finally received a letter from Bird. He explained that he needed my money to keep the business running, but that he would pay me two months' wages the following month. Month after month passed without a single check from Bird. Without me, he was having difficulties keeping the service station running properly, and as a consequence, I was never to receive the money for my education.

To support myself and continue with school, I needed to find a part-time job. Jimmie, for some reason which he refused to tell me, either could not or would not find work for himself. Since his family never sent any money for expenses, I had to cover all the food and rooming costs for both of us. After a few months of this, I could not continue at Chaffee. My educational skills were too low to struggle through the classes, and my expenses were too high for me to make ends meet.

Thus, in only a few short months my dream of a college education was interrupted. Regretfully, I dropped out of school to regroup and decide what to do next. I left Jimmie on his own and took a full-time job at Torley's Market in Ontario, determined to earn enough money so that I could return to school as soon as possible.

This setback at Chaffee made me more determined than ever to get an education. I was disappointed by this experience but not defeated. I had made the trip to California, which I felt certain was a step in the right direction, and above all, I still had my dreams.

There are no defeats, only momentary delays. It is important to keep your goals firmly in mind and to continue to pursue them.

7.
Torley's Market

T he owner of Torley's Market was a heavyset man, standing over six feet tall. He had an aggressive, intimidating nature and kept his employees in a state of apprehension with his constant barrage of sharp, gruff orders.

Torley was my boss, but I was hired initially by the branch manager at the market in Ontario. He was a pleasant man, humble, where Torley was loud and threatening; a pleasure to work for, where Torley was a nuisance. My first job in the Ontario market was in the produce department. I spent my days arranging fruit and vegetables for display, enjoying my work and the people I met at the market. I always arrived at the store early and stayed after closing time to help the manager clean up.

Soon after I started working at Torley's, he opened a new market in Pomona, a town about six miles west of Ontario in the direction of Los Angeles. I was given a better paying job at this new market as a grocery cashier, but I now found myself under the cold and watchful eye of Mr. Torley himself. My promotion, then, was a mixed blessing.

I had been working the cash register for only two weeks, becoming familiar with the prices of the various items and getting to know the customers, when I ran into a problem. As a cashier, I learned that I was expected to place packages of older fruit and vegetables or other items that needed to be moved from the market in with the customers' groceries. All the cashiers were required by Mr. Torley to add one or two items of unwanted goods with each large order of groceries. Generally, the customers failed to catch the additional cost added to their total purchase. If anyone should happen to notice or to return the extra merchandise, we were told to apologize for our "little mistake" and give them a refund or credit. The other cashiers complied with Torley's orders, stifling their complaints for fear of how Torley might respond. But I could not. As this dishonest practice went completely against my beliefs, I did not charge the customers who went through my line for items they had never intended to purchase. Consequently, at the end of the day, while the other cashiers had unloaded their basket of marginal produce onto unwary customers, my counter was still full of unwanted goods.

It didn't take long for Torley to discover what was going on. "What is this?" he demanded in his booming voice. "Why don't you sell this food like I told you to?"

I thought that what he was doing was dishonest, and for that reason I refused to take part in his schemes.

Torley was upset. He looked at me first in disbelief and then in anger.

"I gave you an order," he said. "You, young man, are working for me. When I tell you to do something, you do it!"

I carefully explained my position again to Torley. I could tell he was getting very angry as I spoke. He was not accustomed to having people stand up to him, especially in front of his other employees.

In his rage, Torley opened his mouth to tell me what I could do as far as my job was concerned. I saved him the breath.

"Torley," I said, "I quit."

I took off my apron, said goodbye to the other workers, and walked away from the market, never looking back.

Stand up for your beliefs. Be true to yourself, for honesty breeds confidence and self-respect —absolute necessities for a successful, happy, and creative life.

8.
More than Just Another Job

A fter leaving Torley's Market, I moved from my old room in Ontario and secured a bed in the YMCA in Pomona. There I met Frank Pedley, Jr. who came to the "Y" to work out in the exercise room and swim laps in the pool almost every day. We soon became good friends.

One Sunday afternoon Frank invited me to his home to have dinner with his family. His father was head of Pomona's water department. When I told how I was fired from Torley's Market, Mr. Pedley offered me a job helping him at the water department. Naturally, I accepted.

It was a great relief to be working again, especially for someone I admired and respected as much as Mr. Pedley. His kindness and generosity helped me in my new job.

The water supply in Pomona was furnished by a system of pumps located in various places throughout town. Mr. Pedley was responsible for monitoring these deep-well vertical turbine pumps, which were connected to storage tanks through a network of pipes. Assisting him in this demanding job, I was required to make a daily check on the amount of water in the storage tanks and to inspect the working condition of each pump and water well.

This was an interesting job and I took my work very seriously, learning as much as I possibly could about deep-well vertical turbine pumps. I spent my days driving around town checking the pumps and the water storage levels. In the process, I discovered how wells were drilled and learned all about underground water resources. Since we used pumps that were manufactured in Pomona, I was able to visit the pump factory and observe the entire manufacturing process.

Though I had no idea at the time, the knowledge I gained working for Mr. Pedley was to play a crucial part in my success later in life. I approached this job as all jobs should be approached. I looked on what I was doing as an opportunity to learn. I concentrated on discovering solutions to the problems at hand and I challenged myself always to find the most efficient means of doing my work.

Meanwhile, the Pedleys took me into their family. I felt at home in Pomona and enjoyed my work. There was something new to learn every day.

As the population of Pomona grew, our responsibilities constantly increased. A larger water supply was needed to meet the demands of the community. Mr. Pedley began taking bids on new water tanks from various sources. Western Pipe and

Steel of Los Angeles, a company that manufactured steel tanks, water well casing and pipe, was one of the major suppliers in southern California. Herb Walters, a salesman for Western, stopped by one day to see about a bid he had made to supply us with our new tanks. Walters had been doing business with Frank Pedley for years, and the two had become good friends.

Mr. Walters invited me to join him and Mr. Pedley for lunch. As we ate, the conversation turned quite naturally to products manufactured and sold by Western Pipe and Steel. Mr. Walters explained to me that his job took him throughout southern California, where he made periodic calls on city water departments, on large farms and ranches, and on various oil refineries. His territory covered most of California south of Santa Maria, a town about halfway between Los Angeles and San Francisco.

"How would this kind of work interest you?" Mr. Walters asked.

I told him that I was interested in water wells and would like to learn as much about this trade as possible.

A few days after our luncheon, Mr. Pedley called me into his office.

"Mr. Walters has set up an interview for you," he said. "You are to meet with Charley Tole, the sales manager for Western Pipe and Steel. Mr. Walters is looking for someone to assist him with sales in his territory, and I recommended you as a possible candidate."

Mr. Pedley thought this job would be a great opportunity for me. The pay was good, the experience priceless, and on top of that, the company supplied its salesmen with a car and full traveling expenses.

I thanked him for what he had done. The next day I went to the interview. It was a success. I took the job.

Life should be a constant quest for learning and growth. Every experience offers an opportunity to acquire knowledge.

9.
Too Much, Too Fast

I was hired in 1938 by Western Pipe and Steel Company as a sales trainee. The company manufactured and sold water well casing, pipe, corrugated culvert, tanks, and specialized fabricated steel products. I accompanied Herb Walters on my first sales training trip.

We visited farms, ranches, refineries and prospective customers throughout southern California. During the trip, I saw some of the most beautiful farm land I had ever seen. The farms and ranches in Oxnard, Ventura, Santa Paula, Carpinteria, and Santa Barbara were so beautiful and productive they seemed unreal — like a too highly colored landscape painting. Row after row of green, growing vegetables on this canvas was made real by the smell of freshly plowed soil. I was thrilled by the sight of the orange and lemon groves with their fragrant blossoms and golden fruit.

When I saw this magnificent, productive soil, I felt sorry for my father and his farming neighbors who were trapped by the Dust Bowl and the Depression. I thought of their struggles as they tried in vain to grow crops on dry, lifeless land, while here, in front of me lay this wholesome soil, brimming over with an abundance of healthy crops.

This rich beautiful land, however, gave me hope and inspiration, especially when I learned from Mr. Walters that irrigation water for these farms was supplied by deep-well vertical turbine pumps from an underground source. Irrigation was the key to the success of California farms. I reasoned that the same could be applied to the high plains areas of Texas. The secret was water. If water could be found underground and brought to the surface, then farming would flourish. I vowed to learn all I could about deep-well vertical turbine pumps, and to return one day to my home state to help establish irrigation farming.

After the trip, we returned home to attend a company sales meeting at the California Club in Los Angeles. The subject under consideration was the present and future business opportunities for Western Pipe and Steel. One item on the agenda was the establishment of a business relationship with the rapidly developing country of Mexico. In order to do this, it was suggested that the company make a bid on the corrugated culvert needs for Mexico's portion of the Pan-American highway. My boss, Charles Tole, stated the company's intentions.

"Realistically," he said, "we have little chance of securing this present corrugated culvert order.

We've never done any business south of the border, but I believe this is an excellent opportunity to get Western Pipe and Steel's name into Mexico for business considerations in the future."

He planned to contact the proper government official in Mexico, and send a messenger of goodwill. Being new with the company, without a definite job, I was selected to hand-carry the bid to Mexico City.

This was my first experience outside of the United States. I flew to Mexico City via Dallas and San Antonio, Texas, presented my passport, and went through customs. I then took a peso cab to the purchasing offices of the Mexican government and was introduced to Señor Antonio Martínez. He was responsible for the purchase of corrugated culvert.

As is the Mexican custom, we spent some time talking and getting acquainted. Señor Martínez expressed an interest in the California school system. He said that he was planning to send one of his sons to school in the United States, and would like to hear my thoughts about California colleges. I told him about my efforts to get a college education and how impressed I was with the quality of the educational system.

As we talked, I indicated my interest in learning more about Mexico. Señor Martínez seemed pleased and suggested that I meet a young niece of his, Alicia García Golán, who worked for the Mexican tourist department. He called her and set up a time for us to meet.

The next three days and nights I was treated to a feast of sights, sounds, and history, as Alicia showed me Mexico City — the cathedrals, the National Archeological Museum, the Opera House, the night clubs, and much, much more. We had a wonderful time together touring this fascinating and cosmopolitan city.

My sightseeing excursion, delightful as it was, had to come to an end. I thanked Alicia for her hospitality and friendship and before heading back to California, I returned to the purchasing office to make a final call on Señor Martínez. I expressed my appreciation for all he had done for me and told him how much I had enjoyed my stay in his country and seeing the sights with his gracious niece. After awhile, our conversation turned to some of the finer points of doing business in Mexico.

"It is customary in my country for the purchasing agent to collect a commission on all of the orders he places," Señor Martínez said. "If Western Pipe and Steel is willing to comply with this established custom, I see no reason to look elsewhere for our corrugated culvert needs. I would like to give you the order."

This would be a great coup for a freshman salesman. I called Mr. Tole in Los Angeles and told him of my conversation with Señor Martínez. He authorized payment of the commission fee for the transaction and I left Mexico the next day with the order in hand.

I returned to California exhilarated over the success of my first business trip. As a first-time salesman, I had secured a major order with the Mexican government that my boss had not expected. Mr. Tole and the other officials at Western Pipe and Steel were delighted with the surprising results of the trip and complimented me heartily on my achievement. In addition, I had made some new friends in Mexico and had had a wonderfully enjoyable time. I was in the highest of spirits and felt on top of the world.

Unfortunately, this early success went straight to my head. During the next three months, I made calls on ranch and farm customers in southern California, but I was unable to settle down to my job. I considered myself, the successful businessman, to be above routine sales work. I became careless with my responsibilities and took my good friend Frank Pedley and his son to San Francisco in my company car without informing my boss, Mr. Tole.

It was a classic case of "big shot-itis," and Mr. Tole recognized the symptoms. Upon my return from San Francisco, I was called into his office for a talk. "Too much success too fast can become a handicap," he said. "Western Pipe and Steel, I'm afraid, can only use one president at a time. You have great potential, Clifford, but you still have plenty of growing up to do."

Mr. Tole suggested that I return to college, as I had originally planned, and gain some more formal education.

With that, I was fired.

Too much success, too fast, can lead to unrealistic expectations. A dose of realism, while unpleasant, is helpful in keeping your feet firmly placed on your chosen path.

10.
Sears, Roebuck & Company

H aving been fired from Western Pipe and Steel, I decided to take Mr. Tole's advice and return to college. I enrolled at Pasadena Junior College. There I met Milt Clark and we became roommates. We rented a room a few blocks from the campus for twelve dollars a month. As soon as my sparse belongings were moved into the room, I hit the pavement looking for part-time work.

I landed a job bussing dishes at the YWCA cafeteria. Working the lunch and dinner shift, I earned twenty-five cents an hour plus meals and occasional tips. All things considered, it was a good job. Food and spending money were taken care of, and the hours I worked left me time to attend morning and afternoon classes. I found time to study after I got home from work each night. My school experience at Pasadena Junior College seemed much easier than at Chaffee Junior College in Ontario. Also it was a relief to have a roommate who was able to pay his share of the expenses.

English was still my most difficult subject. However, I found the assigned reading list to be stimulating and enjoyable. I especially remember the passage in Lincoln Steffens' *Autobiography*, in which he writes about taking his young son out to show him a leaking water faucet. He explains to his son that there are unlimited opportunities in the world. Man has not even learned how to build a good water faucet. This example stimulated my thinking and I came to the conclusion that every product, system, idea or concept can be improved.

I continued to bus dishes at the YWCA until the Christmas school break when I found a job at Sears, Roebuck & Company. It was a position in the stock room which paid more than my restaurant work. Tommy Wright, the stockroom manager, agreed to give me part-time work that wouldn't interfere with my school classes.

One of my new responsibilities was to straighten up the stockroom, something that had not been done for a long time. The place was a mess. It was extremely difficult to find the required merchandise for the various departments in the store. Time wasted searching for supplies in the stockroom meant poor service at the retail end. I decided to make some changes.

I put my plans down on paper with the stock organized in both alphabetical and numerical order. I divided the merchandise for each department in such a way that items could be easily and quickly identified when needed. Because my plan was both simple and efficient, Tommy granted me permission to go ahead and make the changes.

One day Mr. Wright brought in another student, Jimmy McCaffery, to help me reorganize the stockroom. I showed him my plans and told him about the changes I intended to make.

As we proceeded with the new layout, I told Jimmy that I thought working in the stockroom was one of the best jobs in the store. I explained that we had the opportunity to familiarize ourselves with all the merchandise in the store and to learn about pricing, labeling, supply sources, and Sears' code for determining how long each item had been in stock. The best way, I felt, for a person to master a business was to start at the bottom and learn the entire industry as he works his way up. In our case, the bottom was the stockroom.

I arrived for work one Saturday morning and Jimmy said that his father would like to meet me. He invited me to his home for dinner.

"What does your father do?" I asked, as we began our work in the stockroom.

"He's an executive. He's the vice president in charge of all west coast operations for Sears."

I stopped dead in my tracks. So Jimmy was the vice president's son! Laughing, I happily accepted Jimmy's invitation.

That evening, we went to his home in Altadena where I met his father. Jimmy had told him about our work in the stockroom and about my interest in the whole operation at the store. I told Mr. McCaffery that I found the job in the stockroom to be challenging and an opportunity to learn a great deal about merchandising.

Mr. McCaffery said that I had been a good influence on Jimmy and that he would like to have me visit frequently. Thereafter I spent a great deal of time at the McCaffery home and joined them for dinner from time to time. The three of us spent hours after dinner talking about Sears stores and ways to improve them. Mr. McCaffery always listened to my ideas and encouraged me to think out loud with him.

One special evening, Mr. McCaffery invited me to a party he was giving for his good friend General Robert Woods, the president of Sears, Roebuck. Mr. McCaffery introduced me to the general as a college student and hard-working Sears employee. Then he proceeded to tell him about my stockroom reorganization and some of my ideas for improving the store. I felt quite honored to be in the company of General Robert A. Woods and yet, at the same time, I felt very comfortable with him.

Shortly after this dinner party, I was called into Mr. McCaffery's office and given a managerial trainee position with Sears. The job paid sixty dollars a month. It required me to work in all the departments of the store, and yet did not interfere with my school program. My hard work and ingenuity was recognized and rewarded.

There are no perfect products, services or systems. Every job offers opportunities to make improvements. Be innovative and express your ideas.

11.
Selling Bloomers

y first weeks at Sears were full of hard work and learning. As a managerial trainee, I was taught the basics of merchandising and all the aspects of retail business. I studied store layout, learning how to analyze the flow of customer traffic and utilize this flow for maximum sales and profit. This included placing the goods we most wanted to move next to the aisles where the floor traffic was the heaviest.

Working at Sears was challenging and interesting. I enjoyed the work and attempted to learn as much as possible from the experience. I looked forward to each day which brought with it new things to learn and new opportunities for me to solve problems.

One phenomenon, unique to this trade, I found of particular interest. On days when Sears advertised a giant sale, hordes of people would gather early in the morning in front of the store, waiting for it to open. At the appointed time, and with great ceremony, the front doors would be thrown open to a thundering stampede. On one such occasion, it was all I could do to jump out of the way to avoid being run over by the press of customers.

Racing down the aisles, shoppers would hunt frantically for sale items that we had strategically placed in out-of-the-way locations. In this manner, customers were forced to sift through regularly-priced merchandise to find the discounted articles they were looking for.

When they reached the sales area display tables, the shoppers, mostly women, were surprised to find that the various items were not in boxes, but were heaped higgledy-piggledy on the tables in a confusion of sizes and colors. This was no longer shopping; this was now a treasure hunt. One time, for example, I watched in dismay as a crowd of ladies charged madly to a display table and began plowing through a pile of bloomers. The bloomers were the hot sale item for the day, and as far as these women were concerned, just about anything went when it came to grabbing bloomers. The ladies jostled one another, trying to find the colors, sizes, and styles they wanted. Little respect, if any, was shown to their fellow shoppers as they mobbed and crowded each other to such an extent that many of the bloomers were left mangled and torn in the wake of the assault. I looked on in bewilderment. It was truly astonishing!

I had been working at Sears for two years and was now finishing my sophomore year at Pasadena

Junior College. One day Mr. McCaffery invited me to meet him at his executive office in Los Angeles. He complimented me on the job I was doing and asked me if I would like to work in his office on a permanent basis. We discussed the opportunities this new assignment would offer. I realized, as we talked, that I had already been thinking that it was time for me to do something else with my life. I had been feeling cooped up and regimented. Homesickness was catching up with me. In the end, I told Mr. McCaffery that I did not want to work permanently for Sears. In fact, I told him, I was planning to move on.

"I'm disappointed to hear this," Mr. McCaffery said. "I've always felt that there was a long and prosperous career for you with Sears. By the way, if you don't mind my asking, what in fact *do* you want to do with your life, Clifford?"

I told him that this was a difficult question — one that I had spent plenty of time thinking about.

"First," I said, "I'm going to return home to see my family and old friends. Then I want to continue my education at the University of Texas. After that, I really don't know yet what I will do."

I paused for a moment and then added, "But I'm sure that I *don't* want to spend the rest of my life selling bloomers to frenzied women."

Mr. McCaffery laughed. "I admire your honesty, Clifford. Be sure and stay in contact with me, and if later you change your mind, I'm certain there will always be a good job for you here at Sears."

It is just as important to discover what you *don't* want in life as it is to decide on what you *do* want.

12.
Homesick and Back to Texas

omesick, without a job, and not knowing what I wanted to do next, I decided to return to Texas. Fritz Biery, a fellow worker and friend at Sears, helped me plan my trip back to the state where I was raised. He offered me a down sleeping bag, filled a knapsack with food, and drove me out to the edge of Los Angeles, where he said good-bye and wished me the best of luck.

Having previously traveled Route 66 from Texas to the Pacific coast, I decided to see some new country on the return trip. I would make my way north through California, turn east, and then south through Utah and Colorado on my way back home.

I hitched rides up the coast and slept in the open air, eating mostly from the food in my knapsack. Along the way, I camped on beaches, in parks, and in the redwoods. I finally arrived in San Francisco and crossed the Golden Gate Bridge on foot. As I reached the northern end of the magnificent bridge, I came upon a large group of students. They were gathered there, milling about, hoping to find rides to wherever it was they were going.

On my trip thus far, I had tried my hand at writing poetry. When I saw all of these students holding up homemade signs that announced their hoped-for destinations, I knew I had to distinguish my placard from the others. I found a piece of cardboard and printed my own sign: "I am a poet." I held up my sign and in no time two young women drove up in a convertible.

"We'll take the poet," they called out to me.

"With pleasure," I said, climbing into the back seat of their car. The three of us took off down the road.

It felt good to be on the move again. I was heading back to my roots and I was charged with the same kind of exhilaration I'd had when driving to the coast three years earlier. Although I had adopted California as my new home, I missed the plains of Texas and looked forward to my return.

We made good time out of San Francisco. The girls, who were students at Cal Berkeley, requested that I quote poetry to them as compensation for the ride. So I recited a poem that I had composed on my way up the coast:

Within our hands we hold
The clay of life to mold,

To free humanity of all
The breathing dead.
To give them life again,
Show them the light of day
And all the beauty that it brings.
Soothe their thirsting lips,
Give to them a sip from
Nature's ever overflowing cup,
Brighten their dulling eyes,
Lift their heads into the sky,
Cast their gaze upon the
Glorious beauty of field,
To know that every hour
Birth is given to another flower.
That God sits quietly by
From his kingdom in the sky,
Or depthward in the sea,
Awaiting the day when man
Will free himself from all his
Self-concocted drinks
And drink from Nature's
Ever overflowing cup.

Within our hands we hold
The clay of life to mold.

We quickly became good friends on the trip, telling stories and talking about our lives. When the girls insisted that I stop in Santa Rosa to stay with their parents, I gladly accepted the invitation.

Their father, it turned out, was an English professor. He was intrigued by my trip and wanted to hear all about it. The two of us enjoyed a marvelous evening talking and discussing poetry. I was especially interested in Walt Whitman at this time in my life, as his poem *Song of the Open Road* fit my mood perfectly:

"Henceforth I ask not good-fortune, I myself am good-fortune,

Henceforth I whimper no more, postpone no more, need nothing,

Done with indoor complaints, libraries, querulous criticisms,

Strong and content I travel the open road."

The short time I spent with Professor Whitehead was to deepen my appreciation and understanding of poetry. That evening, I gained new insights into the wonderful poems in *Leaves of Grass*. It was the poet Walt Whitman's masterpiece, his life's work which the great Ralph Waldo Emerson described as "the most extraordinary piece of wit and wisdom America has yet contributed." Together, Professor Whitehead and I recited these poems aloud and discussed their meaning.

Next morning, I awoke with the sun, feeling young and strong and high as could be. I was "... healthy, free, the world before me ..." inviting me to enjoy its beauty.

I thanked my hosts for their wonderful hospitality, bade my new friends good-bye, and was once again on my way to Texas. I set out on foot, walking along a secondary highway, all the while looking for a ride. Eventually a farmer picked me up and we moved off down the road to the east. At no time in my entire life had I felt so content, so elated, and so completely in tune with the world, as I did at that time.

As we sped off down the open road, the farmer broke the silence between us with a question.

"Where 'ya headed?" he asked me.

I quickly responded with the same poetry of Walt Whitman's that I had heard the night before and which was still chasing around in my head.

"I will go where I please, 'The long brown path before me leading wherever I choose...'"I said, quoting directly from *Song of the Open Road*.

The farmer looked at me, surprised and even angered by my innocent, lighthearted response.

"You're trying to tell me," he said accusingly, "that you don't even have a destination?"

"Of course I have a destination," I said. "Only, it keeps changing. It changes almost every day."

Suddenly the farmer veered his pickup to the side of the road and ordered me to get out.

"You bum," he said. "You should get yourself an honest job. Settle down and start earning a living."

And with that, he pulled away from the shoulder and left me standing alone in the gravel. The road stretched out empty and endless in both directions as far as I could see. I tried to come to grips with the elation I had been feeling only moments before, compared to the utter bewilderment that now overcame me.

Life, I saw, was full of contrasts. Only the night before, Professor Whitehead had encouraged me to continue on my present path, living the life of the open road, and now, the very next day, I was verbally attacked for doing so by some redneck farmer I hardly even knew. I thought about the words of Thomas Wolfe, "... the world is made up of only two kinds of people, the put-er-inner and the take-er-outer." Obviously the irate farmer considered me a take-er-outer, but I knew that I was and always would be a put-er-inner.

I forged on, nevertheless, ready at every turn to meet with more of life's ups and downs. I finally arrived back in Hart, Texas, where I spent two weeks in my old home town, visiting with friends and getting reacquainted with the surroundings. I stopped to see Bird Cox, and he promised again to send the money that he *still* owed me. Some things never change.

I had now come full-cycle back to the place where I was raised. However, I knew in my heart, and probably had known secretly all along, that Hart, Texas, was no longer the place for me. I had to come home to confirm this. I now knew for sure that I had dreams and aspirations that reached far beyond the borders of this little farm town.

So once again, as I had done only a handful of years before, I left Hart behind me, its people and dusty plains held forever in my memory.

Growth and change are vital for a healthy, successful life, but it is important to review and retrace our steps to make sure we have chosen the right path.

13.
Church or Dance

T homas Wolfe wrote that "you can't go home again." This was certainly true for me. I left Hart a second time, traveling with my good friend, Leroy Aven, to Austin with plans to attend the University of Texas. The money Bird Cox promised to send me again failed to materialize, and try as I might, I was unable to find adequate employment in Austin to cover the costs of tuition and living expenses. So I took to the open road once more, heading this time for Houston.

In Houston, I found a cot at the YMCA and a job at a clothing store. I made friends with Vince Floyd, and together we joined a young people's class at the First Methodist Church, where we met the president of the class, J. H. Freeman, who was to become a lifelong friend. We were introduced to some other outstanding young men and attractive young women. During a program for the class one Sunday, I gave a presentation on Emerson's *Essay on Self-Reliance*. It went over extremely well, and I was asked to present the same talk to the general church membership.

It was there that I met Dr. Paul Quillian, pastor of the church. After my presentation on Sunday, he invited me to his office to become better acquainted. He asked me what I was doing and what I planned to do with my life. I told him that my long-term plans were uncertain, but for the near future, I hoped to attend the University of Texas at Austin.

"Have you considered Southern Methodist University?" he asked me. "They have a fine theology department there."

"No," I told him, "I would prefer going to the University of Texas. I would like to study there for a year or so before deciding what direction I want to take."

"Oh, I see," said Dr. Quillian, smiling, as if he had heard words to the same effect from young people many times before.

I continued to visit Dr. Quillian whenever I had the chance and attended church each Sunday to hear him preach. He was an intelligent man and an inspiring speaker who was fond of using stories to put across his message. His interpretation of Christianity gave me a new and fresher look at life.

One of his stories which made a lasting impression on me was about two bricklayers who were working side by side. One of the men seemed gloomy and appeared to be taking no pleasure in his work.

The other man worked with joy, laying the bricks with an air of satisfaction. A passerby noticed the workers and stopped to ask what they were doing. The gloomy man answered, "I am working hard trying to make a living laying these damn bricks." The second bricklayer looked up at the passerby and answered, "I am building a cathedral."

On one of my visits to Dr. Quillian, he suggested that I go back to the University of Texas and take up theological study. He offered personally to help with my financial needs. I accepted his offer and returned to Austin at the beginning of the school year in 1940. Dr. Quillian sent letters on my behalf, introducing me to Dr. Heinsohn, the Pastor of the University Methodist Church, and Dr. Hall, the head of the Wesley Foundation on campus. I was a student once again!

I thoroughly enjoyed my days at the University of Texas. It was there that I met Ray Pollock. He was from Dallas, the son of a Methodist lay leader. Ray and I became instant friends. We were both in Dr. Hall's Bible class and attended church together each Sunday. During our school days, we spent countless hours in conversation. I told Ray all about my life in Texas and about my travels to California and back. I told him about Dr. Quillian and his wish for me to study theology at S.M.U. We talked about what we hoped to accomplish in our lifetimes. We were together when Dr. Heinsohn, on the recommendation of Dr. Quillian, suggested that I serve as president of the Wesley Foundation, a student body organization with high social and educational goals.

The Wesley Foundation was housed in a beautiful stone building on campus, adjacent to the Methodist Church. Dr. Hall was in charge of the Foundation's numerous programs.

As president of the Wesley Foundation, I immediately began working on some social goals. Ray and I came up with a few ideas for developing a new program. To begin with, we initiated a "home away from home" program on campus. Any student who felt lonely or left out of campus life was encouraged to drop by on Saturday evenings to become acquainted with other students in the same situation.

The women of the church endorsed our plan wholeheartedly and helped out by supplying our gatherings with coffee, soft drinks, and cookies. The students enjoyed the camaraderie at their home away from home and were eager to expand the program. With the help of Dr. Quillian, who sent a phonograph machine and some records at my request, we started to hold dances, which were well attended and enthusiastically received.

To meet the growing needs of our program, Ray and I organized a central leadership committee. Twelve members made up the committee, whose job, among other things, was to come up with ideas to assist other students at the university. Many of the students came from extremely poor families and had difficulty supporting themselves in college. As even part-time work was hard to come by at this time, many students relied heavily on outside assistance to stay in school. Having experienced this hardship myself, I wanted to help these students as best I could.

To help defray costs, we organized a "House of Commons" where students at the University could live together and share expenses. We rented an old fraternity house, fixed it up, and hired a part-time cook to prepare our meals. We then invited any student who lacked adequate housing to be our guest — to eat with us and to sleep on one of the couches at the house. The students assisted us with the daily chores around the house and contributed in other ways.

The program was running smoothly. I wrote Dr. Quillian and told him about our activities. He was very pleased. He encouraged me to continue with the progam and offered financial help.

Then one day, I received a call from Dr. Heinsohn. He asked me to stop by his office. He explained that it was against the rules of the church to hold dances on church property. From now on, we would no longer be permitted to hold our popular Saturday evening parties. Social gatherings were perfectly acceptable, but no more dances.

I told Dr. Heinsohn that I would discuss this with Dr. Quillian and my Committee of Twelve and then report back to him. The committee met the following day to discuss the dancing issue. Because we thought the rule was outdated and unnecessary, we decided unanimously to continue our program. Dr. Quillian, a progessive theologian interested in increasing young people's involvement with the church, was also in favor of our decision and encouraged us to continue.

We held another dance.

The following week, I was called again by Dr. Heinsohn, this time to attend a meeting of the Board of Deacons at the church. Resisting any moves toward social change, the traditionalists on the Board insisted that we put a stop to the dancing. I tried my best to explain that from what we had learned in our studies, dancing was well within the teachings of the Bible. My theological arguments did not move them. The Board of Deacons was in charge, and when the Board said no more dances, that meant no more dances.

Our Committee of Twelve met again and decided to disregard the demands of the Board. We felt justified in what we were doing and that there was really no reason to discontinue the dances.

The Board of Deacons was upset with our decision. Dr. Hall asked me to resign as president of the Wesley Foundation. Ray Pollock was offered the position, but my good friend refused the assignment.

As if all this weren't trouble enough, I discovered that Martin Dies — a congressman from Texas and the Chairman of the Congressional Committee to investigate communist activities — was currently investigating *me* and *my activities*!

When informed of this, Dr. Quillian came out to Austin immediately. He spoke with Dr. Hall, Dr. Heinsohn, and with Congressman Dies. During their conference, Dr. Quillian let it be known that he was in complete support of our program to help students financially and include them in the social and educational activities of the church.

Nonetheless, Congressman Dies continued his investigation. There was considerable discussion around the university about the subversive House of Commons and the Committee of Twelve, but in the end, Congressman Dies concluded in a public statement that I was one of the most "American" young men he had ever met. As far as he was concerned, I should be thought of not as a morally subversive individual, but rather as a constructive young Christian leader.

When it was all over, I thanked Dr. Quillian for his unstinting help. I told him, however, that I no longer was interested in studying theology. I was still uncertain as to what I wanted to do in the future, but for now I planned on returning to California. I assured Dr. Quillian that no matter what I decided to pursue, I would always try to live by Christian principles, as I understood them, and try to build cathedrals rather than just lay bricks.

Dr. Quillian was sorry to see me leave, and I was sad to say good-bye. These were the truly formative days of my life, and he had been with me all the way. With his support and encouragement, I gained confidence in myself and the strength to go on through the tough times of growth and change ahead. During my church and school days, I learned one of life's most important lessons — to get involved, take a position, and not to be afraid to stand up for your beliefs.

I was now ready to return to my adopted home of California. It was time to take a new direction again — to live, to learn, and to grow. I packed my few belongings, my books of poetry by Whitman, Tennyson, and Thomas Wolfe's novel *You Can't Go Home Again,* along with Emerson's *Self-Reliance,* and set off for whatever adventures awaited me in the West.

Hold firm to your deeply held beliefs. You will be rewarded with self-respect and the loyalty of true friends.

Section Three

EARLY BUSINESS

"Nobody made a greater mistake than he who did nothing because he could only do a little."

— Edmund Burke

14.
Starting at the Bottom

itchhiking from Texas back to California, I was fortunate to catch a ride with a young couple who had purchased a new Packard automobile in Detroit. We enjoyed our trip to the coast, stopping along the way to explore the countryside and historical landmarks.

Back in California, which was beginning to seem more and more like home to me, I was invited by my friend Fritz Biery to stay with his family in Altadena until I found a job and a place to live. Fritz, who was still working for Sears, Roebuck & Company, suggested that I return to work for my old company. I was broke and needed a job, but I did not want to go back to Sears. The Japanese had just attacked Pearl Harbor, and I was anxious to find a job in the defense industry.

One morning just after dawn, I borrowed Fritz's bicycle and rode south towards the industrial section of Alhambra. I was riding along Fremont Street when I noticed a group of people lined up in front of an iron gate outside some industrial buildings. I stopped and asked one of the men why he and the others were standing in line. He told me that a company called "Lights, Incorporated" was interviewing people for jobs starting at ten o'clock.

It was early in the morning but I decided to stay and try my luck at a job. I got off my bike and took a place in line. At ten o'clock the line of people began moving steadily forward. It was soon my turn for an interview.

"What kind of work are you looking for?" the hiring agent asked.

"I'll take the lowest paying job you have to offer. I need the work," I said.

"Come on in. We can use you."

I was overjoyed. This was a low time in my life. I was out of work, without a home of my own, and more or less alone in the world. I needed to start somewhere, even if it was at the bottom.

Early the next morning, I arrived ready to work and was put on the assembly line. It was my job to attach straps with brass rivets to round steel rims. We were building portable runway lights for the Air Force. These packaged lights were to be air-dropped to our military forces behind enemy lines so that our engineers could set up night landing strips on which our planes could land after dark. My pay was fifty cents an hour.

I found manual work both satisfying and enjoyable. I had worked with my hands almost all my life, and this job was easy for me. However, during my first day on the line, while holding a rivet in place, I struck my finger with a hammer and bruised it quite severely. Afraid that this accident might make it difficult for me to do my job, I got permission from my boss to stay after work to devise a way to work with an injured finger.

Hunting around the shop until I found the tools and materials I needed, I constructed a wooden jig which would hold the rivets in place and allow me to get on with my work. I left the shop feeling good about solving this problem.

I was up early the next morning ready to try out my new jig. I got myself set up on the line before any of the other workers arrived. The jig was an amazing success! It held the rivets in place, freeing one hand and making it possible for me to accomplish more than I could by the previous hand-held method. My boss came by and complimented me on my new jig and the work I was producing.

With the jig I could finish my work on the line about twice as fast as before, leaving me plenty of spare time. I asked my boss for additional work, and was assigned a number of odd jobs around the shop. I helped some of the women on the line, adjusting their work stools to a more comfortable height at which they could be more productive. I assisted my boss in every way possible. I always came to work early in the morning, and stayed after work to help clean up and organize the shop for the next day. It was a good job and satisfied my needs at that time.

The people at Lights, Inc. were like a family to me. I became involved in the company's recreational activities. They had a softball team that played once a week against other small business teams in the area. I became co-manager of the team. It was on the dusty baseball diamond out behind the plant that I met Orin Harvey. He was captain of the team and purchasing agent for Lights, Inc. We became good friends, and one day at practice, we got to talking about our jobs.

"How do you like working for the company?" he asked me.

"It's a good job," I said, "but I'm becoming bored with riveting rivets. I'd like to find something more challenging to do, something where I can learn more."

A few days later, Mr. Harvey came out to our production line.

"How would you like to work in the purchasing department as an order clerk, Clifford?" he asked me. He went on to explain the duties of an order clerk and told me that he felt that I could learn a great deal about the company's entire manufacturing process by working in purchasing. He emphasized that all materials that go into the end products were handled by the order clerks.

I liked the idea. My present boss, however, was pleased with my productivity and was reluctant to let me go. But after some straight talk about my waning interest in shop work, he agreed to let me move on.

I found my new job — ordering material for various aircraft lights and related items — to be very interesting, and Orin Harvey was an ideal boss. He listened attentively to my suggestions for improving the department and encouraged me to pursue each of my ideas. Given this freedom, I created a new, more efficient purchasing system which vastly improved the flow of materials to our subcontractors. I listed the quantities and specifications of the materials for each product we manufactured on an individual order sheet, thus making it possible for our clerks to simply multiply the items on the product sheet by the number needed when ordering materials. This did away with the complicated and frequently faulty purchasing system of the past.

Even with my new system, problems still arose when the engineering department altered the specifications without notifying the purchasing department. I therefore suggested to Mr. Harvey that we establish a planning group under his direction to work with the engineers to guarantee that all specification changes were posted up-to-date. My plan was implemented, and proved to be quite useful.

Under the ownership and leadership of Thayer Thorndike, Lights, Inc. achieved national recognition. The company became known not only as an excellent aircraft and airport lighting manufacturer, but also for its system of subcontracting. Lights, Inc. was one of the first companies to receive the coveted Army and Navy E 2-star award. *Time* magazine ran an article hailing "the amazing firm of Lights, Inc., which has gone and done one of the most vital jobs in the war effort: to make subcontracting really work and really pay."

My own hard work and problem-solving abilities were recognized and rewarded. Within a year after starting as a fifty-cents-an-hour assembly line worker, I had moved into the purchasing department and had then become assistant manager of the P.B.A. (Portable By Air) landing lights division. Shortly thereafter, I was appointed Director of Industrial Relations and Assistant to the President.

My new responsibilities were a considerable challenge to me because of my limited educational background. I decided to continue my quest for education by enrolling in an evening industrial relations class at Cal Tech. This experience stimulated my thinking. After discussing evening educational opportunities with my associates, I decided to establish a company educational program and encourage all interested employees to participate. Arrangements were made for our employees to attend evening classes at the three major educational institutions in southern California — Cal Tech, USC and UCLA. We also conducted classes at our plant during the day and in the evenings. This program became an enjoyable and worthwhile experience for our employees and the company benefited from their heightened productivity.

Mr. Thorndike supported these innovations. There was an area, however, in which he did not care to involve himself, and that was in the field of public and community affairs. Therefore, in a sense, he subcontracted these responsibilities to me, his new assistant. I became a member of the Alhambra Rotary Club, the Chamber of Commerce, and helped organize the Junior Chamber of Commerce.

As the war drew to a close, Paul G. Hoffman organized the Committee for Economic Development to help facilitate the transition from a wartime to a peacetime economy. I was appointed chairman of the Alhambra committee. We developed a program which was recognized and used as a model for other communities throughout the U.S.A. Paul Hoffman and I became good friends and worked together on various projects for the rest of his life.

Much can be said for starting at the bottom without recommendations or inside contacts. There is no better way to learn the fundamentals of a business and gain the necessary self-confidence to move on in that business or another.

15.
Cutting Red Tape

ne day, at the age of six, I wandered out to the corral at my grandfather's ranch and climbed onto a horse named "Spooks." The name fit the animal's character. He threw me off and my right elbow was crushed in the fall. Because there were no doctors in the area, my arm was wrapped in brown paper soaked in vinegar, bound, and put in a sling until it healed. Since then I have suffered a stiffness in my elbow.

My stiff elbow resulted in a 4F classification during World War II, which prevented me from serving in the military. At the time, this was a depressing blow to a young patriotic Texan. Therefore, I did all I possibly could to contribute to the war effort at home.

Shortly after I started working in the purchasing department at Lights, Inc., I was given an opportunity to prove my usefulness. One day my boss, Orin Harvey, asked me to straighten out a difficult procurement problem for the company. With great determination to succeed, I went to work.

Lights, Inc. had taken an Army contract to produce some electrical harnesses for the M-10 guns our soldiers were to use on the European front lines. We were unable, however, to purchase the cable to the Army's specifications. The cable called for had been produced during World War I and was no longer available. We had located a new and improved cable which was superior to the one specified, but when my boss tried to get the Army to change its specifications, he ran into a tangle of red tape. In frustration, he delegated the job to me. I did everything possible to get the necessary changes made, but military bureaucracy being what it was, my attempts drew little response.

Meanwhile, Mr. Thorndike called Harvey into his office to ask why we were not delivering the electrical equipment. The Army, Mr. Thorndike said, was threatening to cancel our contract and find another company to supply the electric harness.

His concern about losing a sizeable order with a customer as important as the U.S. Army was quite understandable. When Mr. Thorndike passed his worries on to my boss, he, in turn, passed them straight on to me. I made a new complete file of the cable procurement problem, including copies of all letters and telegrams sent to the Army procurement office, as well as a log of the numerous phone calls.

One morning, at Harvey's insistence, I took my files and went to Mr. Thorndike's office to explain the situation. I had never met Thayer Thorndike before. As I walked down the hall to his office, however, I was eager to discuss this matter with him. I had done my homework and despite our previous frustrations, I knew exactly what was needed to solve the problem.

I entered his office and spotted Mr. Thorndike seated at a large conference table with four Army officers dressed in medal-bedecked khaki uniforms. At the head of the table sat a colonel. The five men looked up as I walked into the room. I nodded, introduced myself, and took a seat.

After a brief moment of silence, the colonel turned to me. "Young man," he said, without formally introducing himself or his fellow officers, "what is the reason for not delivering on this vitally needed material? Don't you know there's a war going on?"

I stared at him in disbelief. Stunned, I was silent for a few moments. Besides the red tape we had encountered with the Army every step of the way, this was absolutely the wrong day to ask me that question. Earlier that same morning, I had received word that my younger brother was in a hospital in London. He had been shot while fighting in action. His condition was unstable.

"Well?" the colonel demanded.

I could no longer hold back my anger. "Yes, I know damn well that there's a war going on. And at least I'm trying to do something about it. If I had your uniform, I would be out fighting the war, not sitting around here asking stupid questions like that."

As I stopped to catch my breath, I felt the glare of five pairs of eyes. I deliberately placed my files on the table. Opening them, I turned to the telephone numbers of the procurement officers responsible for the contract changes, and showed them to the colonel.

"If you will pick up the telephone on the table in front of you," I said, "and call your buddies at Army Purchasing to get the authority to change these specifications as we've been recommending for some time now, I'm sure we could have the materials flowing immediately."

The colonel seemed surprised by my bold behavior, but he took my files and checked our recommended changes. Then he made the call and read the specification changes over the phone, and as easy as that, the problem was solved.

I stood up and started to leave the office. Before I reached the door, however, Mr. Thorndike stopped me. He asked me to join the group for lunch where I had the opportunity to apologize for my sudden outburst at the meeting.

A few days after this incident, Mr. Thorndike called me into his office. "Sit down, Cooper," he began. I was unsure how he would respond to my forthright behavior in front of the officers. As I took my seat, I prepared to defend my actions.

"What you did the other day took courage," he said. "You knew that you were right; you had done your homework, and you were not afraid to voice your opinion. I admire that in a man, Cooper. I'd like to make you my assistant. It will be your job from now on to help me expedite solutions to company problems."

I accepted his offer.

Sometimes it is difficult to solve problems in a complicated bureaucratic system. A simple, direct and even blunt approach will often work, but you must first be sure of your facts.

16.
A Handshake Partnership: Big T Pump Company

I met Boyd Kern, the president of Wintroath Pumps, while I served as secretary of the Alhambra Rotary Club. I assisted him in club matters during his term as president, but we also frequently discussed the pump business and the benefits of irrigation farming, so that when he invited me on a business trip to Arizona, I gladly agreed to join him.

We stopped frequently along the way to visit with California farmers who were using Wintroath pumps on their land. In Arizona, we met cotton farmers and had the opportunity to inspect a vast wealth of citrus groves. At our final destination, the company's Phoenix office, I had the chance to view its extensive pump repair and service facilities.

On the return trip to California, Mr. Kern asked if I would consider joining Wintroath Pumps as his assistant. Ever since working for the Pomona City Water Department and Western Pipe and Steel, I had become interested in deep-well vertical turbine pumps. It wasn't the pump business itself that held my interest so much as the virtual certainty that these pumps could help transform farming. After seeing the rich and productive irrigated land in California, I visualized equally abundant crops and lush farms springing from the dust of the Texas Panhandle.

As we sped through the quiet desert, I asked Mr. Kern if he would consider expanding his pump business, as he had done in Arizona, to include Texas and her neighboring states. He weighed my question carefully before answering.

"If an affordable and profitable market could be found in Texas," he said at last, "then, yes, Clifford, I would certainly consider expansion." With those words in mind, I accepted his offer to join the Wintroath Pump Company.

Shortly after I became Mr. Kern's assistant, the two of us took a second business trip. This time we traveled to Texas and the Midwestern states with the purpose of looking into possible pump sales. Along the way we stopped at a Santa Fe Railroad office where we learned that an ample supply of underground water had been found at train stops all across the high plains. The water we needed was right under our feet, just waiting to be tapped. An abundant source had been found at depths of between 60 and 250 feet below the ground, an easily accessible range for the pump technology currently employed in California.

Encouraged by this promising discovery, we

stopped in Hereford, a small town in the heart of the Texas Panhandle and the county seat of Deaf Smith County. I introduced Mr. Kern to my good friend Leroy Aven, and the three of us went to visit some Hereford farmers. We learned that irrigation farming had already been attempted, and that the wells had failed miserably. Although there was plenty of water, the wells were unsuccessful because of inadequate drilling and a lack of pump servicing and technical know-how.

These problems could be solved, but another more serious obstacle stood in our way, and that was financing. After meeting with a Hereford banker to discuss the possibility of lending money to the farmers to purchase our pumps, my optimism was greatly diminished. If dry land farmers were unable to finance their pumps, then irrigation farming could not become a reality.

"All these dry land farmers know how to do," the banker drawled, "is get on their knees and pray for rain."

Unfortunately this banker's ignorance was not limited to unbecoming social prejudices. He went on to cite the lack of reliable well-drilling capacity and pump service facilities, as well as the community's general lack of irrigation farming knowledge. His reasoning was based on failed attempts of the past rather than on an intelligent organized approach to the present situation. I was frustrated not only by the banker's narrow scope of vision, but also by his negative attitude. With my belief that wallowing in the negative is no way to approach a problem, I cut the banker off between complaints, said good-bye, and walked out of his office.

I suggested to Mr. Kern that we establish an office and service department in Hereford similar to the one we had visited in Phoenix. We could locate reliable well-drillers and arrange a line of credit with the Bank of America at our California headquarters, thus enabling Wintroath to finance the farmers' pumps. Mr. Kern wanted to discuss this proposal with his board of directors before he committed himself. Back on the coast, I prepared a detailed written outline of our plans for Mr. Kern, but despite my efforts, the board of directors voted against establishing a facility in Hereford. Mr. Kern apologized to me, explaining that the company was short of working capital and was in no position to invest in a Texas facility. He had decided, however, to give me the opportunity of putting together an organization of my own to sell and service Wintroath pumps in the Midwestern territory. He offered me a 5% distribution contract with the exclusive right to establish pump dealerships in all states except California and Arizona. The pump dealers would receive a 20% discount off the recommended sales price. I would be strictly on my own, though, without salary or expenses.

I had been in this position before, and even in the same geographic area. The Runt Pig Principle had worked then, and I believed that it would work for me again. A contract was drawn up and signed.

With a supply of pumps from Wintroath, I could establish pump dealerships, provide service facilities, bring in well-drilling capacity, and arrange financing. I could put together a complete irrigation system, creating a reliable and economically feasible supply of water for the dry land farms. I visualized that everyone involved would benefit and that a new and prosperous economy would evolve. The Dust Bowl poverty on the high plains would be eliminated. It was now only a matter of solving the problems and creating value.

Immediately after signing the distribution contract, I called Leroy Aven in Texas. I explained the deal with Wintroath and asked him to meet me in Hereford the following day.

I took off in my Hudson automobile down Highway 66, the same road I had traveled some ten years earlier when I left Texas to attend school in California. Much had happened since then and I had learned a great deal both in school and at work. I felt ready for the big challenge, but knew that I needed Leroy as my partner. Leck, his father, had taught me the important lesson of matching. Leroy and I, like a perfect pair of matched mules, knew how to work together.

I arrived in Hereford the next day after driving over a thousand miles without sleeping. Leroy met me in Ike's Cafe, the only restaurant in town. After an early supper, I checked into the Long Horn Motel to get some rest.

The next morning at breakfast, Leroy and I started planning our business venture. I suggested that we organize a Hereford dealership and call it "Big T Pump Company." Big T would be the first Wintroath Pump sales and service dealership in the Midwestern territory. We shook hands and agreed to be fifty-fifty partners.

We had a great number of problems to solve. We needed a building large enough to accommodate our new pump dealership. I needed a distribution headquarters with a warehouse, and a shipping-receiving office. While Leroy looked into the purchase of a plot of land at the edge of town on Highway 60, I traveled sixty miles northeast to Amarillo to investigate some war surplus steel buildings that the government had up for sale.

I found the buildings all packaged and ready for overseas shipment. The price was right, so I wrote a check for $3,400 to purchase two buildings, each measuring 40 x 80 feet, and left instructions for them to be delivered to Hereford. This purchase depleted my bank account, but I felt confident in what I was doing. Meanwhile, Leroy borrowed $1,000 from his father to make a down payment on the land, which cost $4,250. Leroy agreed to assemble the buildings when they arrived. We were now ready to set up shop.

I took off the next day for California, feeling good

about the beginning of our business. We had gotten started, which is often the most difficult step to take. I knew that Leroy would make good progress setting up Big T. Now it was time for me to get down to solving the more difficult problems of locating financing and establishing pump dealerships in the Midwestern states of New Mexico, Texas, Oklahoma, Kansas, and Colorado.

I had a lot of time to think on my way back to the coast. As the miles of paved highway disappeared under my wheels, I began reviewing my experiences over the past ten years. I soon realized how many of those seemingly unconnected events in my life would help me now with my program to bring modern irrigation farming to my homeland. There was my experience at the Pomona water department, where I first learned about pumps. Then my job at Western Pipe and Steel showed me the success of irrigation farming in Oxnard, Carpinteria, Ventura, Santa Barbara and other parts of California. I felt sure that the same methods of irrigation farming could be adapted to the Midwestern states as well. My business experiences at Lights, Inc. taught me the importance of subcontracting to keep overhead and investment low, and of bringing together and utilizing outside resources to develop finished products. My managerial training at Sears, Roebuck & Co. gave me a basic understanding of merchandising, advertising and business fundamentals. I remembered the last thing my friend and employer, Mr. McCaffery, had said to me when I left Sears. After wishing me good luck, he'd said he would be happy to help me in the future if he could. Sears could be the answer to my big, complicated problem of pump distribution. With McCaffery's help, I could establish Sears, Roebuck farm stores as pump dealers throughout the Midwestern states. Sears could sell pumps, along with their other farm machinery and supplies, to farmers on credit and thus solve the critical financing problem.

I met with Mr. McCaffery and presented my proposal, which he liked. He suggested that I take my ideas to Chicago and speak with General Robert Woods, the president of Sears.

Having met General Woods at Mr. McCaffery's home some years before, I had no trouble getting an appointment to see him. I went to Chicago and presented my plan for selling pumps and bringing irrigation farming to the Midwest, explaining how this would dramatically improve the economy, and subsequently increase sales and profits for Sears stores. He saw the value of my plan, but said that the territory I wanted to serve was not covered by Sears, but by its main competitor, Montgomery Ward. He volunteered, however, to set up an appointment for me with Sewell Avery, the president of Montgomery Ward. General Woods informed me that Mr. Avery was very conservative and not inclined to take risks on new products and concepts. He wished me the best of luck, saying I would probably need it.

I met with Mr. Avery the following day and presented my plan to him. He listened, looked me over carefully, and then finally asked, "What kind of discount does Wintroath offer on their pumps?"

I knew from General Woods that Mr. Avery would be adamant about receiving at least a 35% discount on all merchandise sold through his stores. I also knew that 20% was the maximum discount I could offer on Wintroath pumps. Therefore, I quickly chose to direct our discussion away from raw business numbers.

"Have you considered the total value you will receive by helping change the high plains into an area of modern irrigation farming?" I began. "The economy will skyrocket. A population boom will follow. And more people mean more money to be spent on all your merchandise. I'm positive, Mr. Avery, that you could afford to sell these pumps to farmers at a break-even mark-up, and still profit from the deal."

I waited for Mr. Avery to reply. While my logic was alluring, he wasn't biting. He insisted again that 35% was the required discount. No less.

We talked the matter back and forth, before he finally agreed to send two of his top staff men with me to look into the market potential of my proposal. I returned to the high plains area with Mr. Avery's assistants. We talked to Montgomery Ward store managers in Dodge City, Kansas; in Clovis, New Mexico; in Amarillo and Lubbock, Texas. We made a general evaluation of the market opportunity for pumps, and then Mr. Avery's agents reported back to him.

The results were favorable. Mr. Avery authorized a purchase order for two hundred pumps, as I had proposed, making this the largest order for deep-well vertical pumps ever placed with Wintroath. This large order thrust Wintroath Pumps, Montgomery Ward and Big T into business in the Midwest territory. Wintroath borrowed needed working capital against the 200 pump order and rented one of Big T's buildings in order to provide a distribution facility in Hereford, Texas. Montgomery Ward sold pumps to the farmers on credit. Local bankers soon started providing financing for pumps.

The dry land farmers learned quickly and soon became successful at diversified irrigation farming. Big T gradually evolved into a full water systems company — drilling wells, assembling pumps, supplying irrigation equipment — and offering complete customer service. Wintroath sales and profits increased so dramatically as a result of the high volume of sales in the Midwest territory that they tried to force a purchase of Big T in order to protect their market. They threatened to cut off Big T's supply of pumps. We chose to remain independent and made arrangements to represent all other major pump companies. Wintroath countered by building a large plant in Hereford and started directly competing with Big T.

At first there was enough business for everyone, but gradually Big T grew stronger, dominating the market. Within less than three years, Wintroath sold their Hereford plant to Big T. As the economy strengthened, Big T went on to become a diversified agro-business, buying and developing land, farming, raising and feeding cattle as well as continuing to sell and service complete irrigation systems. The Dust Bowl conditions and the poverty they created were eliminated. The high plains turned into one of the most productive agricultural areas in the United States.

If you believe in something and you feel committed to it, stick with it. Look around to see what resources are available to you. Analyze all the needs and your ability to satisfy them. Then go for it!

17.
Shorty Ware: Water Witch

I n 1946, when I began my program to establish Wintroath pump dealerships in the Texas Panhandle, it became necessary for me to locate some good well drillers. I let word out that I was looking for well drillers with equipment capable of drilling wells 16-inches in diameter and down to as much as 400 feet deep. Here's how we found one of them.

I got wind of a driller in Muleshoe, Texas, a small farm town just forty miles south of Hereford. Having grown up in a farming community, I was familiar with the peculiarities of small-town living. I had a hunch, for instance, that if I were to call the phone operator in Muleshoe, she would not only know of this man, but would more than likely know where and how to find him. (One of the benefits of rural living was the forty-line phone system which made the local operators privy to all the news and gossip of the town — a privilege that small-town operators everywhere were apparently born and bred to use to their fullest advantage.)

I called Muleshoe from my office in California and got the operator on the line. I asked her if she knew of Shorty Ware, the well driller.

"Shorty... 'course I know Shorty. Everyone knows Shorty," she said in her easy-going, slow-as-summer drawl. "And I'll bet ya, Honey, I know right where you can find him."

I declined the bet, but found out that at that hour of the morning Shorty would most likely be working on a hot meal at the local town cafe.

"If you'll hold the line, Honey, I'll ring up the White Face and see about ol' Shorty."

So she called the cafe and I listened in on the conversation at the other end of the line. A waitress answered.

"Honey," said the operator, "'Shorty there?"

"No, Shorty ain't here right now," came the waitress' cool reply.

"Honey, don't Shorty take his breakfast at your place?"

"No, he don't eat here no more, but he does have a cup of coffee every once in awhile."

I thanked the operator for her trouble. I asked her to leave word that I wanted to talk with Shorty if she could get ahold of him, and I gave her my name and number. A few days later, I received a call from Muleshoe.

"Honey, I've got Shorty on the line for you."

I talked briefly with Shorty, the well driller. We made arrangements to meet on my next trip to Texas.

When I arrived in Muleshoe, I stopped by the White Face Cafe to get directions to Shorty's home, which happened to be on a farm close to town. Shorty lived with his brother Leonard, a well respected farmer in Muleshoe. I met with Shorty and he let me take a look at his drilling equipment. He had an old Fort Worth spudder drilling rig, a good piece of equipment, but certainly not capable of drilling a well large enough or deep enough for our needs.

While we were talking, Leonard came in from the fields, and Shorty introduced us. I told the two brothers about my plans for building a distribution center in Hereford to supply pumps to farmers for irrigation. I explained my need to develop a water well drilling capacity for a 16" well-casing down to maybe 400 feet. The Ware brothers were very interested in what I had to say.

During our conversation, Shorty told me that he was a "water witch." A water witch, as I already knew, was someone who could locate underground water with nothing more than the aid of a forked stick. I was somewhat skeptical of Shorty's claim, but Leonard, who seemed to be the brighter of the two, vouched for his brother's mysterious talents. He insisted that Shorty was so good at his trade that he could find water in the ground faster than a lonely bull could find a way to keep himself occupied in a herd of cows. How could I argue with that?

I suggested that the two brothers take a trip with me to California and look over some new well drilling equipment that had the capacity to drill straight wells large enough and deep enough for our needs.

"Cal-i-fornia!" they echoed in unison.

The clincher was when I mentioned that I would introduce them to Rosco Moss, the most successful well driller in California. The smiles on their faces nearly filled the room.

Shorty and Leonard drove to Hereford with me, where I introduced them to my partner, Leroy Aven. The brothers then followed me to Alhambra, California, where they met my business associate, Mr. Kern. I took them on a tour of the Wintroath Pump factory. We then drove to Los Angeles and I introduced them to Rosco Moss. The three men talked for a long while, sharing tales of legendary drilling experiences and then struck a deal on a new rotary well drilling machine, which was promptly shipped to Muleshoe.

With their new equipment, the Ware brothers became two of our most successful well drillers. Leonard handled the business affairs, while Shorty concentrated on the actual drilling and water witching. With a green forked stick grasped firmly in each hand, the talented Shorty walked around the surface of the farms until one or both of his sticks pointed at the ground, revealing the location of hidden water sources. These brothers from Muleshoe were perfectly matched and could work together.

Our business was beginning to boom and my dream of pumping water to farm dry lands was steadily becoming a reality. Some credit for my successful operation must be given, however, to the Muleshoe phone operator who so graciously helped me put together the Ware Brothers' Drilling Company.

Thank you very much, Honey.

When making a deal, negotiating a trade, or establishing a business relationship, try to make arrangements that benefit all parties involved.

18.
Harvesting Pipe

T he Big T Pump Company, born with a handshake between my good friend Leroy and me, began to grow and prosper. Well-drillers and other pump companies moved to the high plains to take advantage of the large vertical turbine pump market we had helped to create. For awhile our pump business was booming. But then, as always seems to happen at the height of prosperity, we ran into a new problem.

Life, I was learning, is full of new problems. No matter how well things are going at any particular time, there's always a problem lurking just around the corner. But after all, it's problems that make life so interesting, and solving them that makes it so enjoyable. In fact, I was beginning to see myself headed towards a career as a problem solver. And so I set out optimistically to clear yet another hurdle standing between me and success in business.

The problem at hand was directly linked to World War II. During the war, larger and larger demands had been put on America's steel companies to produce more and more ships, planes, tanks, and armaments. Consequently, the nation's steel supply had been depleted. The steel industry had not been able to produce enough material for commercial use.

We had most of the components necessary for a complete pump assembly, but one essential item was in short supply — standard lapweld pipe. The farmers had already purchased their pumps. Wells had been drilled. But without the pipe, the pumps could not be installed. The time for planting the year's crops was drawing near. Soon the land would need water, and if we could not find lapweld pipe, and find it quickly, the farmers would lose a full year of crop income. Most of the farmers could not afford the loss of a full year of productivity. Unless the pipe was found, all the work we had done trying to bringing water to the Dust Bowl would be lost for at least a year.

We tried every possible pipe supply source throughout the United States, but could not find what we needed. Then one morning, while I was out driving, I passed by some old oilfields. It occurred to me that all the old shallow oil wells in Texas and Oklahoma, which had been pumped dry of their oil, contained miles of used pipe. Why not pull out this pipe and see if it could be adapted to our pump needs?

Like the useless slop and grain fed to my runt pigs, the unused oilfield pipe could be put to a new and profitable use. We gave it a try and discovered that the pipe was available in the sizes we needed. The pipe was of excellent quality, having been coated and protected with crude oil for years. We had the oilfield pipe pulled up and delivered to our yard in Hereford. Much to our delight, even after the expense of cleaning, it cost much less per foot than new lapweld pipe.

The problem was solved. The oilfield pipe was not only less expensive than new lapweld pipe, but more importantly, we were able to supply complete pump assemblies for our waiting farm customers. They, in turn, were able to produce profitable crops for the year.

When the solution to a problem is important to you, be creative. Explore substitutes and alternatives. There is usually an answer to every problem.

THE LIGHTS' BEAM

NUMBER 1
VOLUME 1

APRIL 1943

A monthly publication to develop cooperation, inspiration and good-fellowship our employees, subcontractors and friends — Lights, Incorporated, Alhambra, C

ON THE BEAM

Today's bouquets go to a chap who is proving the saying, Where there's a will —there's a way. This ambitious young man started on the assembly line with Lights, Inc., just a year ago. In this short period of time he has advanced from the Purchasing Department to Assistant Manager of the P.B.A. Division. From there he has just recently been promoted to Director of Industrial Relations where the vast knowledge he has gained through the various departments will be of tremendous value to his success in his new position. Good luck to you, Cliff Cooper.

The Amazing Growth of Lights Incorporated

ERNEST W. DUXBURY
W. M. C. Instructor

CLIFFORD D. COC
Director Industrial Re

University of California
at Los Angeles

University of Southern Califor

California Institute of Technology

Industrial
EDUCATIO

Cliff Cooper rising through the ranks at Lights, Inc., 1943.

Portable-by-Air (PBA) landing lights ready for shipment to Europe.

Employees of Lights, Inc. receiving Army and Navy "E" metals from Cliff Cooper, Director of Industrial Relations, for contribution to the war effort.

Paul Hoffman, Chairman of the Committee for Economic Development, and Cliff Cooper, 1944.

Letter from Paul Hoffman to Cliff Cooper regarding Cliff's appointment to the Alhambra Committee for Economic Development.

Committee for Economic Development

285 MADISON AVENUE · NEW YORK 17, N.Y.

RECEIVED
JUL 22 1944
LIGHTS

July 17, 1944

Mr. Clifford D. Cooper,
Director of Industrial Relations
Lights, Incorporated
1111 South Fremont Avenue
Alhambra, California

Dear Mr. Cooper:

Mr. Asa V. Call has advised me of your appointment as Chairman for the Alhambra Committee for Economic Development. I am delighted to know that you have accepted this responsibility.

Every member of the Board of Trustees feels as I do — that satisfactory progress in the postwar period can be made only if the problem of maximum employment through expanded production is tackled on a company-by-company basis in the community.

You can count on receiving the full support of the Committee for Economic Development in this important work you have undertaken.

Sincerely yours,

Paul G. Hoffman

Paul G. Hoffman, Chairman
The Board of Trustees

/ez

Texas Panhandle farmers viewing a Wintroath pump display at Montgomery Ward's.

Cliff Cooper and a Montgomery Ward store manager demonstrating a Wintroath pump in Plainview, Texas.

One of the first Wintroath pumps installed by Big T Pump Co. in
Hereford, Texas.

Open ditch irrigation with siphon tubes.

Typical row irrigation of cotton near Petersburg, Texas.

National Grain Sorghum Producers

After irrigation, abundant crops of sorghum grain were harvested on the high plains of Texas.

Section Four
THE LEADERS

"No man is good enough to govern another man without that other's consent."

— Abraham Lincoln

19.
General Eisenhower

T he year 1947 was very busy for me. My time was occupied in helping Leroy establish our Big T pump business. Organizing pump sales and service programs for Montgomery Ward in five Midwestern states, as well as setting up independent pump dealerships for Wintroath Pumps in Texas, New Mexico, Oklahoma, Colorado, and Kansas kept me on the move. In addition, I was elected vice president of the United States Junior Chamber of Commerce.

One of my responsibilities as vice president was to attend state Jaycee meetings throughout the country. Fortunately, I was assigned to the Midwestern states where my business attention was already focused.

On my first visit to Kansas, I met Glen Muncy, a successful wheat farmer and president of the Kansas Jaycees. He invited me to attend the upcoming state meeting in Wichita and asked me to deliver the keynote address. I had been planning to spend time in Kansas anyhow, working with Montgomery Ward farm store managers. I was pleased to accept Glen's invitation. He also informed me that he was going to visit Governor Frank Carlson in Topeka and wanted me to accompany him. The next day we drove to the capitol building where we met the governor in his office. He was a bright and energetic man who enjoyed sharing his knowledge and experience in politics with aspiring young men. On the day of our visit, the governor had received some big news.

General Dwight D. Eisenhower, the World War II military hero, was flying home to Kansas from his N.A.T.O. headquarters in Europe. His visit happened to coincide with the state Jaycee meeting. The governor, who was making welcoming arrangements for Eisenhower, suggested that Glen invite the general to say a few words to the young men of Kansas at their Wichita meeting. Glen informed the governor that General Eisenhower had already been invited.

Ike would be an especially important guest. Not only had he been raised in Kansas, but rumor had it that he might run for president of the United States. Word was out that President Truman wanted to persuade Ike to run as a Democrat. But Governor Carlson saw things differently. Kansas was a Republican state and the governor, a Republican, was doing all that he possibly could to counter Truman's idea by encouraging Ike to run as a member of the Grand Old Party, as any true Kansan should.

Much to our pleasure, Governor Carlson asked Glen and me to join him at the airport to greet General Eisenhower. While waiting for the general to arrive, we had the opportunity to meet a number of politicians and business leaders, as well as Milton Eisenhower, the general's brother and president of Kansas State College.

When I was introduced to the general, he smiled and shook my hand, giving me his complete attention for the moment. The welcoming group accompanied him to his hotel where he was to take a short rest.

We later visited Ike in his hotel room. Glen gave him a copy of the Jaycee program and he seemed genuinely pleased to be speaking to the young men of his home state.

During the course of our conversation, Ike turned to me and suggested that the two of us had something in common. For once in my life, I was utterly speechless. What could I possibly have in common with a five-star general, a legendary war hero, and a possible presidential candidate?

"Well, Clifford," the general said, "on my trip from the airport to the hotel, your friend Glen Muncy pointed out that while Harry Truman is trying to draft me to run for president of the United States, the Kansas Jaycees are trying to draft you to run for president of the United States Junior Chamber of Commerce. "

The meeting in Ike's room eventually broke up and I next saw the general the following day at the state Jaycee meeting. I was honored with a seat at the head table. General Eisenhower was seated at the center of the table, flanked on either side by Governor Carlson, Milton Eisenhower, Glen Muncy, and me.

Throughout the evening, General Eisenhower conversed easily with all of us. To me, he was the epitome of a wise and competent leader. He carried himself with great dignity, and yet there was a warmth in his manner. After listening to him during dinner, I took Glen aside and suggested withdrawing my own speech to give General Eisenhower adequate time to speak and answer questions from the floor. As it turned out, the general needed very little time to put across what he wanted to say.

Standing, Eisenhower faced the enthusiastic crowd. He smiled his familiar, engaging smile and began by saying something like this, "There seem to be two of us seated at the head table being drafted to run for president. I understand that the young men of Kansas want to draft Cliff Cooper to run for president of the United States Junior Chamber of Commerce. At the same time, someone in Washington, D.C. has suggested that I run for president of the United States."

"I don't know what Cliff intends to do," Ike continued, "but I can tell you all tonight that I am not giving any consideration to the suggestion of my own candidacy."

A buzz of excitement rippled through the audience at this unexpected statement, but Ike quickly silenced the chattering crowd by raising his hand.

"Now, gentlemen," he said, "I would like to say a few words to you about what I plan to do after I leave my present military career." We all waited as he paused and carefully collected his thoughts. He went on, saying something like this, "Now that the war is over, I plan to encourage our young men and women to engage in battle against the many problem fronts in America today. I would like to see us establish new beachheads in an effort to eliminate some of our pressing social ills. I would like us to attack the pockets of poverty, establish a better educational system, and create a freer, more competitive economic system that will give each new generation greater opportunities for successful living.

"I don't want to see our country continue sending our young men into battle to be sacrificed. It is my greatest hope and dream," he added, "that we can build a society that will make war obsolete."

General Eisenhower's final words were met with thunderous applause. Standing there with the others as we cheered this great leader, I was so touched by the hopes he had expressed, that I could not hold back my tears. I will always remember his remarks, so simply spoken. Here was a great military leader who understood the costly destruction of war, and who wanted to spend the rest of his life working for peace.

For the first time in my life I had met a man with the capability and compassion to be a fine president of our country. I became aggressively committed at that time to help nominate and elect Ike president of the United States. Three years later, I organized the Committee for Young Men in Government, which established a national organization to assist in the nomination and eventual election of Eisenhower. I had the pleasure of working with Governor Carlson, Sherman Adams, and my good friend Paul Hoffman, as well as most of the leaders of the Republican party, but it would be another five years before General Dwight Eisenhower would take the oath of office to become the thirty-fourth president of our country.

My presidency, however, was much closer at hand. In 1949, I was nominated and elected president of the U.S. Junior Chamber of Commerce.

Active participation in service organizations, such as the Jaycees and Rotary International, will give you the opportunity to develop lasting friendships. You may also have the good fortune to meet inspirational leaders.

20.
Santa Claus to President

I was living in Pasadena in 1943. Christmas was in the air. Single, away from my family and old friends, I had the Christmas blues. The *Star News*, our local newspaper, ran an article about the Santa Claus program sponsored by the Junior Chamber of Commerce. The organization needed Santas and helpers. A meeting to be held at the Pasadena Playhouse that evening sounded like a possible blues-chaser to me. There I met Marvin Lee, the program chairman.

We were organized into teams of three — a car driver, a Santa's helper, and a Santa Claus. On Christmas Eve, the teams fanned out to distribute toys to needy children in the poorer sections of the city. We were armed with maps, along with the names and addresses of the children to be visited. With my helper by my side and bells ringing, I'd bounce out of the car, a sack of toys on my back. Taking a quick glance at my list I'd call out the children's names, along with a hearty ho, ho, ho. After giving toys to the wide-eyed children and wishing merry Christmas to the family, I was off to another stop. We returned to the Playhouse to enjoy a late meal and to share our evening's experiences. This turned out to be the perfect antidote to loneliness and one of the more enjoyable Christmases of my life. Apart from the fun of the evening, I'd made some new friends, including Marvin Lee with whom I've maintained a lifelong friendship.

I soon became active in the Pasadena Jaycee chapter and was appointed dean of the Action College for Practical Knowledge, a leadership training program which met weekly.

Marvin invited me to go with him to the California State Junior Chamber meeting to be held in Santa Barbara. There at a lively Saturday evening reception and dinner, I met the state president, Roger Deas. The next morning he outlined the program for the day and asked each of us to join one of several round table discussion groups.

I sat down with the public relations committee, thinking that I could learn something of value. Roger strolled around to each table, and while at ours, he saw that our chairman had failed to show up. He asked me to lead the discussion and report to the general meeting when we were finished.

That evening, we had our final dinner meeting at which Roger delivered an inspiring speech about the activities and opportunities for service in the Junior Chamber of Commerce. I was stirred by his speech and went forward to tell him so. Roger took me aside and thanked me for helping with the discussion group and for my report. He asked if I would be willing to serve as the California state public relations chairman. I was so impressed by the meeting and his speech that I accepted on the spot.

After returning home, I began to wonder what I had taken on. I realized that I did not know enough about the Junior Chamber of Commerce to be an effective chairman. I called Roger to tell him how I felt and asked how I could get some information on the Jaycees. He suggested that I write to the U.S. Junior Chamber of Commerce headquarters in Chicago, requesting some background information. I received two large mailings of historical material and current committee activities. I organized the data so that I could come up with a statement about the organization's activities, goals and objectives.

As state chairman, I was called upon by local Jaycee chapters to give talks to their organizations. I discovered that the community of Alhambra, where I was working for Lights, Inc., did not have a Jaycee chapter. This was right in my own backyard. At our next Pasadena chapter meeting, I asked if we could organize an Alhambra chapter. I agreed to serve as co-chairman of the organizational committee and to start contacting eligible prospects to join. We soon became an effective service organization made up of some of the community's outstanding young men. I was elected vice-president charged in part with setting up an Action College for Practical Knowledge on the Pasadena model.

Henry Kearns, national vice-president of the Junior Chamber, came to speak to our charter night banquet. As master of ceremonies for the evening program, I introduced him. He later suggested that I become a candidate to serve as a Jaycee national director. I was elected and appointed chairman of the U.S. Jaycee public relations committee.

Earlier, in my efforts to learn about the Jaycees, I'd collected a great deal of information. Now, as national chairman in 1946, I felt it would be a good P.R. tool to produce a 25-year history of the Jaycees. I wrote and published a complete history, detailing many of the community activities sponsored by the Jaycees. I included pictures of all past national presidents, as well as current state presidents, national directors and committee chairmen. The Silver Anniversary History was well received and enabled me to make many friends throughout the country. I presented leather-bound, engraved copies to President Harry Truman, state governors, and leading business leaders.

The next year at the at Long Beach convention I was elected a national vice-president, and many assumed that I would run for president the following year. My business commitments, however, were substantial. We were establishing Big T Pump Co. in Hereford, Texas; I was organizing a Midwestern distribution network for Wintroath pumps; and I was involved with a training program at Montgomery Ward stores to service, sell, and finance pumps for farmers. With these responsibilities, I felt that

I would not have the time required of a president. This appeared to be the end of a most enjoyable and worthwhile experience.

My good friend, Paul Bagwell, was elected president instead. I attended his convention in Philadelphia with some feelings of regret that it would be my last Jaycee national meeting. But events have a way of snowballing.

A few years earlier, the U.S. Jaycees had decided to move from Chicago to Tulsa, Oklahoma, and to construct a war memorial headquarters. Previous efforts to raise the necessary funds had been unsuccessful. President Bagwell asked me if I would be the national fundraising chairman during his term. He promised that he would make raising the funds to build the headquarters his number one objective. I visualized that this would be an excellent opportunity for me to make a lasting farewell contribution to the Jaycees, and I agreed to take the assignment.

We organized an architectural contest and invited young architects between the ages of 21 and 35 to submit their renderings. A financial goal was established and the deadline was set to raise the needed funds before our next national convention in Colorado Springs. I organized a large fundraising committee which included all current state presidents. A Bucks for Building campaign was launched with the objective of getting every member to give one dollar to the fund. We offered a prize of recognition to the state president who achieved the highest percentage of membership participation. Monthly reports were sent to the state presidents showing them their standing in the contest.

Our promotion paid off and we met our financial goal. The architectural submissions were ready to be judged in Colorado Springs. With a great sense of accomplishment, I was ready to attend the convention, enjoy myself, and say good-bye to my many Jaycee friends. Then I could go home, attend to my business affairs and participate in local community activities. Or so I thought.

Back in Alhambra at the first Jaycee meeting after reaching our financial goal, I met my friend, Herb Klein, associate editor of the *Alhambra Post Advocate* and one of our most effective community leaders. Herb told me that a great number of my friends wanted me to run for president of the U.S. Jaycees. This surprised me because I thought it was clear that although I appreciated their support and confidence, I couldn't spare the time for such a major responsibility. Herb persisted and said that he was sure the Alhambra and Pasadena, as well as California, Jaycees were ready to endorse me. He suggested that I give the idea a few days thought.

I called my friend and partner Leroy Aven to ask his advice. He said he'd be glad to see me become a candidate. Big T, he said, was in excellent shape and he could manage our business as long as we stayed in contact by phone and I stopped by now and then as my schedule permitted. Most of the basic problems in supplying pumps to the Midwestern territory had been solved and Montgomery Ward's training program was completed.

In the meantime, Herb had probed around and found that we would indeed have considerable support for my candidacy. It was pretty compelling and I did an about-face and told Herb that if Alhambra, Pasadena, and the California state organization endorsed me, I would agree to be a candidate.

Next we turned our thoughts to the political challenges of winning the election. Three vice-presidents from the Solid South had announced (George Baird from Louisiana, Bev Burbage from Tennessee, and John Hamrick from South Carolina). Not being a vice-president at the time and running in a field of four, I knew that I had much to overcome. One thing working in my favor was the location of the convention in the West. Colorado Springs was in the heart of my major Midwest and Western support. Action, not talk, was needed. We were late and had a lot of catching up to do. Herb put together an effective campaign committee and arrived in Colorado Springs two days before the convention. We set up campaign headquarters in The Antlers Hotel and proceeded to contact the Jaycee leaders and their delegations as they arrived. We arranged to meet with state delegations as soon as possible. However, we chose not to spend our time and energy with Southern states, knowing that our chances of getting their support was very slim with three Southerners in the race.

As the campaign progressed, we picked up strong support in the West and Midwest along with the two delegate-rich states of Ohio and my home state of Texas. Kansas, the first state to endorse me, brought a sizeable band from Ellinwood, which marched and played at every opportunity, hoisting a KANSAS SUPPORTS COOPER sign. A large delegation from San Francisco organized a glee club, which composed and sang songs promoting me. The Hereford, Texas, Jaycees brought their homegrown beef, put on an old time Texas barbecue, and served everyone their natural fluoride water. (Hereford, the home of Big T Pump Co., was known as "the town without a toothache.")

The three Southern candidates became so alarmed at our blitz that they combined their political forces to support one candidate, John Hamrick. This move tightened the race and I did not see how we could win.

We called a meeting of all our supporters to analyze our present position and determine our strategy. Dutch Keslar, president of the Ohio state organization, a tireless and effective campaigner, suggested that we boldly invade the Solid South. He had a plan. The Alabama state president was his close friend. They had served in the war together and were sharing a hotel room during the convention. Dutch proposed that he try to arrange a special caucus with the Alabama delegation and have me make an appearance. Alabama was not only a key Southern state, but it had a great psychological advantage in the electoral process.

The Junior Chamber elections were conducted in much the same way that national political parties nominated candidates for president. The number of voting delegates each state received was determined by the number of its local chapters and members. Therefore, the larger states, like California and Texas, had larger blocks of votes. The states voted alphabetically, which gave Alabama the opportunity to nominate a candidate first, or pass to any state of its choosing. This made Alabama's support most desirable. Historically, Alabama had always voted with the South, but when Dutch arranged an Alabama caucus for me to attend, I discovered much more support than I had expected. I shook hands with each delegate and answered all of their questions. As I walked from the room, Dutch asked me if I would be willing to let his friend place my name in nomination for president if he was able to deliver his state's support. I told Dutch that if the deal could be made, the answer would be yes.

A special outdoor barbecue dinner was planned for the evening before the election. The convention committee had requested that there be no political demonstrations during the evening. However, just as the cocktail hour was getting started, the Alabama delegation burst onto the scene, carrying large signs proclaiming ALABAMA GOES FOR

COOPER. They made a beeline for me and hoisted me onto their shoulders and marched around the gathering of stunned delegates. Feeling somewhat embarrassed, I was at the same time elated to think that my election the next day was almost assured.

The next morning the delegates gathered and the dramatic roll call of states began. Alabama started by placing my name in nomination. The vote was close right up to my home state of Texas. Their delegation permitted the Hereford club to cast the winning vote for me and I became the 29th president of the U.S. Junior Chamber of Commerce.

The next week I was the first president to move to Tulsa for my year in office. I saw the new war memorial headquarters started and close to completion before the end of my term. Santa Claus' gift to me was one of the most stimulating, educational and enjoyable years of my life.

Seek out opportunities to contribute to community, state and national affairs. Be useful and helpful to new friends. Compensation may exceed your expectations.

21.
Harry S. Truman

O ne of the privileges granted me as president of the United States Junior Chamber of Commerce was a visit to the White House to meet the president. In 1949, Harry S. Truman occupied the Oval Office.

Truman, the thirty-third president of the United States, who came to office upon the death of President Roosevelt and who was re-elected in 1947, accomplished a great deal during his two terms in office. He established the Central Intelligence Agency; was responsible for the Berlin airlift of 1948; instigated the Marshall Plan for economic recovery in western Europe that same year; and was instrumental in forming N.A.T.O., the collective security agreement among non-communist countries.

Despite all of these achievements, I did not expect much of our coming meeting. First of all, I had always been a staunch Republican and Mr. Truman was a Democrat. Moreover, I had been working hard to advance the recommendations of the Hoover

Commission during my term in office, and although the commission had been created by Congress under Truman, he had apparently taken little interest in its success.

I arrived in Washington, D.C. by plane. Flying over the city, I could pick out the U. S. Capitol, the Washington Monument, the Lincoln and Jefferson Memorials, and the Smithsonian Institution. The capital city, built in accordance with an original master plan, with its impressive buildings, wide streets, fountains, monuments, and parks, presented a most beautiful and inspiring aerial view.

I was picked up at the airport in a limousine and chauffeured directly to the White House, where I was cleared through the security gates. Before entering the Oval Office, I was advised by the White House Appointment Secretary to keep my conversation brief. The president was a very busy man, I was reminded, and I could have only ten minutes to spend with him.

I entered the Oval Office and shook hands with the President of the United States. Mr. Truman, I observed, was larger in stature and held himself more impressively than I had expected. Following our formal introduction, Truman began showing me around the room, pointing out his numerous trophies and awards. He then turned to show me a plaque that had been conveniently placed on his desk.

"Clifford," he said, "as you can see, I have even

been made an honorary member of the Junior Chamber of Commerce."

"Mr. President," I said, apologizing for my interruption, "we only have ten minutes to talk. I had hoped I could ask you some questions."

President Truman stopped and listened.

"Are you in favor of the Hoover Commission's recommendations?" I asked him.

"Why, of course."

"Then why," I asked, in my usual straightforward fashion, "don't you do more to support them? You have the power and authority to make many efficient, cost-saving changes."

"What would you suggest I do?" Truman asked.

"From what I understand and believe," I said, "you could save the taxpayer quite a bit of money by terminating half the federal jobs in Washington. And doing so, I believe, would make the government run not less, but *more* effectively."

The president frowned. "Have a seat, young man. You obviously don't understand the workings of our government. You are unable to see what would and would not be good for our country. The decisions a president must make are more complicated than you think. Let me try to explain."

He then gave me a short talk on political science. He explained the three separate departments of government — executive, legislative, and judicial — and pointed out that it is the Congress which makes laws and appropriates funds to implement them. The president, he went on, must try to cooperate with Congress in an effort to solve important problems. He suggested that I continue my efforts to get the Hoover Commission recommendations adopted through Congress, as it was Congress that must take legislative action before changes in efficiency and economy could be achieved.

President Truman and I ended up talking together well over thirty minutes.

I left the Oval Office with a new impression of President Harry S. Truman. He was warm and friendly, and yet was possessed of a strong personality and an honest sense of leadership which I came to respect.

As I was leaving the White House, a newspaper reporter approached me. He was interested in hearing about my conversation with the president. I told the reporter about our discussion on the Hoover Commission's recommendations. I outlined our entire conversation and mentioned how I had gained a great deal of respect for President Truman.

The reporter busily scribbled down every word I said.

Much to my surprise, the next day the newspaper ran the following headline in big, bold letters: <u>Cooper Recommends to Truman that He Fire Half the People in Washington!</u>

The following year, Richard Kimler, a Democrat, replaced me as president of the United States Junior Chamber of Commerce. Like myself, he had the honor of paying President Truman a visit. Immediately after their meeting in the White House, Dick called and told me the first thing the president had said to him when they shook hands in the Oval Office.

"I'm pleased to meet you, Mr. Kimler," Truman had said, "and I'm sure glad you got rid of that little black-haired bastard you had running your organization last year!"

Strive to be honest. Speak your mind, for mutual respect comes from honest and free communication. Although it is important to hold your own opinions about a person, avoid being too quick to make judgments.

22.
Judging Miss America

"Return to Atlantic City immediately. We need your help judging the Miss America Pageant!" I received the telegram in Anchorage, Alaska, where, as Jaycee president, I was touring a military installation.

I couldn't believe my good fortune! I knew little about the duties of a judge, and even less about the Miss America Pageant, but I was more than eager to learn. This was one opportunity I wasn't about to let slip away.

I apologized to General Twining, my host at the Army post, for cutting the tour short. The general fully understood my position. He only wished he had been the one to receive the telegram. I bade him farewell and booked the next flight to Atlantic City. During the overnight flight, I used most of my time, sleeping and awake, dreaming about what was in store for me when I reached New Jersey.

I was met the next morning at the airport outside Atlantic City and driven to a hotel and shown to a spacious suite provided by the pageant directors. They suggested that I relax and rest up for the following morning when I would be eating breakfast with a dozen of the contestants. All the judges followed this procedure, meeting personally with the young women before the formal competition.

As I rested my flight-weary body by the pool, I took the opportunity to read up on the Miss America Pageant. Created in 1921, this national event was in its twenty-eighth year. Each year, an estimated 200,000 people throughout the United States donated over six million hours of their time to bring off 3,000 state and local preliminary contests. More than 70,000 young women competed locally, while an estimated one hundred million people watched the pageant on television each year.

It was quite an honor to participate in such an impressive event. As I basked in the Jersey sun, I marveled at how a poor farmer's son from Hart, Texas, could get himself involved in some of these things. Whoever would have dreamed I would be judging the Miss America Pageant? But here I was, ready, as always, to face the challenge of the moment.

During my travels around the United States that year, I had already met and talked with several of the state winners. Miss New Mexico, a bright and beautiful young woman, dreamed of going to college. Unfortunately, she came from a poor family and feared she might never attain her educational goals. Miss California, a lovely blonde from my home state, hoped to make her career in acting; with her bubbly personality, sharp intellect, and bathing suit beauty, she had everything in her favor.

But so did the other women I had previously met, such as Miss Indiana, Miss Mississippi, Miss Georgia, Miss New York City, Miss Oklahoma, Miss Texas, and the sloe-eyed Miss Hawaii. An accomplished hula dancer of Japanese and Hawaiian heritage, she was an exotic beauty.

Before the contest began, I must admit, I was already developing a soft spot in my heart for Miss New Mexico. Because we shared similar backgrounds and educational goals, I hoped she would somehow win the chance to go to college and pursue her dreams. Then again, Miss Hawaii had a special gracefulness about her and would be hard to beat in the overall judging. And, there was Miss California, whose suntanned healthy good looks certainly made her a worthy competitor. And . . .

On the second day, we were briefed on the objectives of the Miss America Pageant as well as on the method of judging. I was impressed by the management of the pageant and their sincere desire to select a Miss America who displayed a balance of personality, character, beauty, talent, and intelligence. The pageant, I discovered, was far more complex than a mere beauty contest. Since the winner would be representing America, she would be in the public eye for a year and expected to uphold the traditions and values of her country. It was crucial that we choose a woman who was likely to live up to these responsibilities.

Following an enjoyable week of preliminary events, the contest finally began. The twelve judges were seated together near the front of the stage where the young women were to model and display their particular talent for singing, dancing or acting. From this vantage point, we could see the contestants' every move.

In the first round of judging, we chose fifteen contestants. From these, we selected five finalists, based on a beauty contest, a talent display, and the answers to personal questions.

When all the votes were finally cast, Miss Jacque Mercer from Arizona was the winner. For her victory, Miss Mercer received a crown, a wreath of red roses, and the honor that came with her new title of "Miss America."

Along with the annual crowning, the pageant also awarded a number of educational cash rewards. In fact, the Miss America Pageant provided more scholarship assistance for young women of college age, about $55,000 annually, than any other private agency in the world. During the various meetings and social events among the judges, I took it upon myself to lobby in favor of awarding Miss New Mexico one of these valuable scholarships. I explained to my fellow judges how Miss New Mexico, raised in a poor family, had always longed to earn a college degree, and that this might be her best or only opportunity to achieve her goal. I was happy to learn, before I left Atlantic City, that Miss New Mexico had been awarded a $5,000 scholarship.

At first, it was difficult for me to see why Jacque Mercer had won the contest; I had failed to take particular notice of her. To my mind, she did not have the most beautiful face or figure, nor was her performance extraordinary, and yet she did well in all categories of the competition. Most importantly, I came to realize, was the way she presented herself. It was in her walk, the way she carried herself, the way she spoke, and her radiating self-confidence that set her apart from the other contestants. She looked and talked like a young woman who was qualified to represent her country, and it was her determination, poise, and sense of purpose that carried her on to victory.

Physical attractiveness is a wonderful asset. However, in order to win a crown, beauty must be balanced with good character, personality, and achievement.

23.
A Lesson in American Politics

E ach year the U.S. Junior Chamber of Commerce sponsors a program to select Ten Outstanding Young Men in America (recently changed to Ten Outstanding Young Persons). These individuals are honored at an awards banquet, one of the Jaycees' most impressive events.

During the 1949-50 term, when I was president, the banquet was held in Peoria, Illinois. That year, we honored a distinguished group of young men. They included, among others, the future president of the University of California, Los Angeles (UCLA), Frank Murphy; a future U.S. Senator, Charles Percy of Illinois; and none other than Gerald Ford, later to become president of the United States.

As Jaycee president and chairman of this recognition program, I was responsible for selecting the keynote speaker for the evening. I was extremely pleased to have my first choice, Paul Hoffman, accept my invitation to speak. I had known Mr. Hoffman for several years. We both lived in Pasadena, California, and I had the privilege of serving on the Committee for Economic Development during the time he headed that organization. In fact, he had encouraged me to run for president of the United States Junior Chamber of Commerce.

Paul Gray Hoffman was a success in both business and politics. He amassed a small personal fortune as salesman, administrator, and eventually president of the Studebaker Corporation. Though a Republican, he was appointed by President Truman to head the European Recovery Program (the Marshall Plan), and was instrumental in helping piece together war-torn Europe. During the latter part of his life, he served seven years at the United Nations, aiding underdeveloped countries.

It was also my pleasure to welcome our second guest of honor, the newly crowned Miss America. Raised on a farm in Arizona, the lovely and talented Miss Jacque Mercer, who claimed both Daniel Boone and President James Polk as ancestors, was as American as the Stars and Stripes. She brought a special grace and charm to this festive occasion and contributed to the success of the evening.

After dinner, the honorary guests were introduced to the business and political leaders who had been invited. A press conference and a major radio broadcast were then held, at which time I gave each Outstanding Young Man a plaque of recognition and asked him to make a short statement. I then introduced Mr. Hoffman, whose speech was instructive and inspiring.

Afterwards, Mr. Hoffman asked me to join him in his hotel suite. He'd flown in a private plane from Washington, D.C. with a group of politicians and business associates, to whom he now introduced me.

"Clifford," he said, "these gentlemen have an interesting proposition to discuss." He nodded to one of the men, who came right to the point. "We'd like you to consider running for office in California with the ultimate goal of being elected governor."

I felt my heart racing as he explained how I would be given all the support I needed in this venture. Adequate finances for my campaigns would be supplied, but I must be most discreet regarding their sources. A considerable portion of the money necessary to finance the campaigns would come from Reno and Las Vegas, Nevada, including generous contributions from Howard Hughes.

"Your friend Mr. Hoffman tells us that you have strong ethical and moral commitments, and that it would be natural for you to oppose legalized gambling, horse racing, and casinos. We would be willing to fund your campaigns as long as you speak out and work against all forms of legalized gambling in California."

A second man in the group added (unnecessarily, it seemed to me) that it was in Nevada's best interest to help elect political leadership committed to eliminating major gambling in California.

It was clear that these gentlemen were concerned that California was beginning to move in on one of Nevada's prime sources of revenue. With horse racing tracks already quite popular in the Golden State, they feared that casinos would soon follow. They were now looking for a way to stop this dangerous threat, and I was being considered as one who might prove helpful.

I thanked the group for their consideration, but the role was not for me. I could not accept the offer. However, if ever I acquired enough support and freedom to run as my own man, then and only then, would I consider running for public office.

The circle of associates seemed to be surprised and disappointed. Mr. Hoffman joined me as I walked out of the room and said that he had felt all along that I would refuse the offer.

"Clifford," he said, "I believe that you would make a great political leader, even on your own terms. I hope to see you elected to public office sometime in the near future."

I was thus introduced to the inner world of politics.

Don't be captured by glittering offers. Being your own person is far more rewarding than being someone else's puppet.

24.
A Dog Named "Hoover"

A s a young boy living in the Texas Dust Bowl during the Great Depression, I owned a black and white speckled dog named "Hoover." The Depression brought poverty and suffering to my family, but my father and grandfather never held President Herbert Hoover responsible for their own hardships. They were great supporters of Hoover and voted for him when he ran for a second term, losing to Franklin D. Roosevelt.

Although my father and grandfather lost their meager savings when the banks closed in 1933, they refused any W.P.A. government assistance during the Roosevelt-New Deal era. My family was stubbornly self-reliant. They would never think of taking free handouts. By one means or another, they intended to work and take care of themselves and their own.

"I will not take money to stand with my foot on a shovel," my father would say, with a proud tilt to his chin. He was referring to the W.P.A. practice of allowing men to check out a shovel at the local W.P.A. office even when there was no work available; when they returned the shovel at the end of the day, they would receive a small stipend.

After President Roosevelt's death, Vice-President Harry Truman occupied the White House. President Truman appointed Herbert Hoover chairman of a commission which Congress created in July, 1947. The commission was to make a study and recommendations for reorganization of the executive branch of government. This became known as the Hoover Commission. Its recommendations endeavored to limit government spending, define executive functions, and make government generally more efficient and economical.

From 1949 to 1950, the year that I served as president of the United States Junior Chamber of Commerce, my primary objective was to stimulate support for the Hoover Commission and to help persuade Congress to adopt the commission's recommendations into law. Visiting all 48 states, Alaska and Hawaii, I delivered an average of two speeches a day in favor of the commission's recommendations.

During the latter part of this period, a group of Jaycees chartered a Pan American Boeing Stratocruiser, named *The Bald Eagle*. It was the maiden voyage of the aircraft. We flew around the world, stopping in twenty-seven countries, in an effort to boost the International Junior Chamber of

Commerce. I returned to Washington in time to lead a large rally on the Capitol steps and to present Vice-President Barkley and Senator Robert Taft with thousands of petitions the Jaycees had collected in support of the Hoover Commission's findings.

As my term in office drew to a close, I continued to focus as much national attention as possible on the Hoover Commission's recommendations. There was no better way to achieve this, I realized, than to have Herbert Hoover keynote my outgoing convention in Chicago. With this in mind, I went to New York to make a call on the former president at his home in the Hotel Waldorf Astoria.

As I entered the lobby of the magnificent hotel, I thought about Hoover's place in American history and how he had failed to receive recognition as a great president. Despite a most distinguished career in private and public affairs — a career which spanned over 50 years and earned him such names as the "Great Humanitarian," the "Great Engineer," the "Great Secretary," and the "Great Public Servant" — his major achievements were sadly overshadowed by that bleak Depression era in American history.

Mr. Hoover was aware of my efforts on behalf of the commission during the past year and received me cordially. His handshake and welcoming smile put me at ease immediately. I asked him if he would do me the honor of delivering the keynote address at the Jaycees' upcoming convention.

He smiled at my request. "Why would you want an old guy like me to speak to your young men?"

I told Mr. Hoover that I, for one, appreciated him as a great leader and respected him as an intelligent, moral man. I told him also that while my family had suffered during the Depression, we never blamed him for the economic conditions in the United States or for our own difficulties.

"In fact," I added, "you might be interested to know that when I was a small boy, I owned a dog that I'd named 'Hoover.'"

The president broke into laughter. "If you promise to let me tell the story of your dog, I'd be delighted to speak at your convention," he said. "After all, Clifford, I know how much every boy loves his dog."

President Hoover came to Chicago in 1950 and opened his speech with the "dog story." When he finished, our young men — who had gathered from Alaska to Florida, Hawaii to Maine and every state in between — stood and cheered for the seventy-six year old former president. The ovation lasted more than ten minutes. There were tears in the eyes of the sturdy men who rushed to the podium in an attempt to carry President Hoover around the convention hall. What a glorious sight it was for me to see the young men of America paying tribute to a great and caring leader of the past. President

Hoover, likewise, was obviously touched to receive such appreciation from me and my generation. The convention was a great success and received the national media attention I had hoped for.

I stayed in contact with Herbert Hoover for the rest of his life. He had a son, Herbert Hoover Jr., who lived in my hometown of Pasadena, and whenever the president visited his son, he always made it possible for me to spend some time with him.

In 1953, President Dwight Eisenhower approved the second Hoover Commission to continue the work of reorganizing the government. President Hoover was again appointed chairman. Upon his request, I served four years on the commission's task force for lending agencies.

Work for causes in which you truly believe. Your efforts will not only advance those causes, but will also allow you to learn and grow. You may find that doors will open to new opportunities and influential people.

General Dwight D. Eisenhower delivers a rousing speech to the Kansas Jaycees, 1947. To the left is Glen Muncy, president, and Cliff Cooper, U.S. Jaycee vice-president.

WWII hero General Dwight D. Eisenhower is welcomed back to his home state of Kansas in 1947. He is met at the Wichita airport by his brother Milton, Governor Frank Carlson, Glen Muncy and Cliff Cooper, amongst others.

Cliff Cooper, Dean of The Action College of Practical Knowledge, a
leadership training program for the Junior Chamber of Commerce.

Santas dressed and ready to deliver toys to needy children in
Pasadena, Christmas, 1943. Cooper is in there somewhere.

J. Allen Hawkins

Breaking the Solid South. Alabama demonstrates for Cliff Cooper and assures his election for president.

Jaycee convention in Colorado Springs, 1949, with delegates from the 48 states, Alaska and Hawaii.

The winning model out of 284 submissions for the U.S. Jaycee War Memorial Headquarters.

Cliff Cooper inspects construction of the new headquarters in Tulsa.

HARRY S. TRUMAN
President, United States of America

*I*t gives me great pleasure to send my greetings to the young, vigorous American businessmen meeting at the Twenty-sixth Annual Convention of the United States Junior Chamber of Commerce.

This country today is faced with enormous problems. At no time in our history have we needed more devotion to country and appreciation of our democratic ideals than now. In your programs of international cooperation and understanding, in your work on community development, in your efforts to promote greater understanding of civic responsibilities, you have made an outstanding record.

I am confident the Junior Chamber will continue to exercise its influence as a dominant force for good government and ethical business relationships. I know the government can continue to count on your group for wholehearted cooperation.

Harry Truman

President Harry S. Truman sends his greetings to the Jaycees in 1949.

Reporter interviews Cooper outside the White House after the latter's visit to President Truman.

Jacque Mercer, Miss America of 1949, with Cliff Cooper and some of the other Pageant judges.

Some of the Ten Outstanding Young Men of America in 1949 in front of their photos, including Gerald R. Ford, Franklin D. Murphy, and Charles H. Percy.

Paul G. Hoffman during an interview, Gerald Ford and Cliff Cooper behind him.

Herbert Hoover reluctantly shakes hands with Martin Kennelly, Mayor of Chicago, 1950.

U.S. JCC President, Cliff Cooper, left, and Ohio President, "Dutch" Keslar, far right, present a big roll of signatures in support of the Hoover Commission Report to Vice President Alben Barkley, left, and Senator Robert Taft, right.

Section Five

TAKING OFF

"Don't part with your illusions; when they are gone you may still exist, but you have ceased to live."

— *Mark Twain*

25.
Hot Rods to Rockets

D uring the year I served as president of the United States Junior Chamber of Commerce, my address was Tulsa, Oklahoma, but my home was the United States and the world. That was a good and exciting year, but now the time had come for me to build a home and establish a new network of business relationships. From the newly established Jaycee headquarters in Tulsa Oklahoma, I returned to live in Pasadena, California.

In the meantime, under the management of my good friend and business partner Leroy Aven, Big T Pump Company in Hereford, Texas, was running well. I served as chairman of the board and was in constant contact with Leroy on all matters relating to corporate policies and major business decisions. Our personal relationship and business philosophy was so much in harmony that we could make most decisions by phone. This gave me a chance to evaluate and become involved in other business opportunities.

One day shortly after I returned to California, Marvin Lee, a good friend of mine, came to visit me in my Pasadena apartment. Lee, a used car dealer who went by the business name of "Starvin' Marvin," had been president of the Pasadena Junior Chamber of Commerce. He was fascinated with racing cars and wanted to introduce me to Wayne Horning, a young man who was designing an engine head for hot rod cars. Marvin asked me to go with him to Glendale to meet Wayne and take a look at his work.

We found him working in a garage behind his uncle's house. The shop was small, yet meticulously clean. Most of the machinery was old and belt-driven, but in fine working order.

Wayne enthusiastically showed us his work and told us that the new head he was designing was in the final stage of development. Marvin then showed me some articles written about Wayne in *Hot Rod Magazine*.

"The kid's a winner," he said.

Wayne smiled and said, "I'm sure I could finish the new engine head in a short time except I've completely run out of cash. I'm paying my Uncle Frank $100 a month for letting me work here."

I asked him how much money it would take to complete his work. Wayne figured that about $2,500 should be enough to carry the project through final development and into production. There was already a great deal of interest, he said, in the new design. In fact, Bob Peterson, the owner of *Hot Rod Magazine*, was following the development of the project and would give the new product plenty of coverage in his tabloid.

We thanked Wayne for showing us his work and returned to Pasadena. The next day, Marvin called and said that he had talked again to Wayne who offered to sell me a fifty percent interest in his new engine head development for $2,500.

That seemed like an intriguing proposition to this new venture capitalist, so I returned to Glendale the next day to work out the business arrangements. I saw to it that Wayne could continue using the garage and machinery for $100 a month. I reviewed his bills payable, set up a new bank account and paid off all his past-due accounts. We shook hands to seal the partnership and in this manner, Horning Engineering Company — located in Uncle Frank's garage on Fletcher Drive — was created.

I was greatly impressed by Wayne and the young men working for him. They worked around the clock and always with the greatest enthusiasm and determination. Wayne was a most remarkable person. While his formal education was limited, his talent and drive were immeasurable. He seemed to me to be somewhat like Henry Ford in his dedication and inventiveness. Wayne took his work very seriously, and yet he could kid about his ability to change hats — wearing one hat for engineering, one for production, one for business, and another for marketing.

While Wayne continued working on the engine head development, I looked around for other business opportunities. If Horning Engineering were to become a successful business, Wayne could manage the company, in much the same manner that Leroy was managing Big T in Hereford, Texas.

After three months of steady work, the new engine head was finally completed. Plans were made and tests were run amidst great excitement and expectation. But the new head failed. We tested it again and again, but it just didn't work.

Wayne was nearly shattered by this failure. He had spent all the available money on this project and had even gone into debt. Utterly discouraged, he was ready to throw in the towel.

In the meantime, I became associated with Soderberg Manufacturing Co. in Alhambra. Fritz Soderberg had purchased the assets of Lights, Inc. and was continuing to manufacture the kind of aircraft lights that we produced during World War II. While working with Soderberg, I made contact with Dave Ireland, an engineer I had known at Lights, Inc. He was now associated with a small group of Cal Tech engineers and scientists who had formed the Jet Propulsion Laboratory.

Dave gave me a tour of the JPL facility which was located in a canyon near La Cañada. He explained the current work of the Cal Tech group and suggested that I might like to explore the opportunities in the relatively new field of solid propellant rockets. As we discussed various applications for solid propellant rockets, the idea of using them to conduct weather research grabbed my attention. I expressed my interest in exploring the possibility of building weather research rockets and becoming associated with the Jet Propulsion Laboratory. I told Dave about my investment in Horning Engineering and our recent product failure. However, I expressed great confidence in Wayne Horning, and felt that he might become interested in building metal parts for rockets.

Dave was impressed by my opinion of Wayne. He wanted to know more about this young man who wore so many hats. JPL was looking for a shop to help build their experimental rockets. He suggested that someone from JPL should stop by and become acquainted with Wayne.

The following week, a JPL employee visited Wayne Horning in the shop and decided to place a small order. Our low overhead (the rent at Uncle Frank's just couldn't be beat) and Wayne's creative abilities made it possible to supply high quality parts on time at competitive prices. Horning Engineering developed a good relationship with JPL and was awarded a continuous supply of orders.

From this small and humble beginning — a mere $2,500 working capital which had been depleted, and zero experience in the rocket business — we launched a very successful company specializing in metal parts for rockets. Within a year, we obtained a contract to build two hundred airframes for a small solid propellant rocket named LOKI. With the profits from this order, we built a new plant in Monrovia, California, and formed Horning-Cooper, Inc.

What began as a failure in the development of a hot rod engine head turned out to be a soaring success in producing metal parts for rockets.

There are no failures — only stumbling blocks on the road to success. Learn as much as you can from your mistakes, and move on.

26.
CDC: Reaching for the Moon

H orning-Cooper, Inc. moved into its new plant in Monrovia and purchased additional machinery. Our business began to grow. We developed a strong relationship with JPL as a result of our ability to deliver quality rocket parts on time and at reasonable rates. We also became associated with a new solid propellant rocket motor company, Grand Central, which had been organized by two former JPL engineers, Chuck Bartley and Larry Thackwell. Bartley and I became good friends. Horning-Cooper furnished Grand Central metal parts for most of their rocket motors.

With a reliable source of solid propellant fuel available in Redlands, California, my dream of building weather research rockets seemed to be closer to realization. I had always been interested and intrigued by weather, having been exposed to its harsh extremes in the Texas Panhandle. I discussed my ideas with my partner, Wayne, and discovered that he did not share my views and aspirations. I tried to convince him that we could succeed in the new field of solid propellant weather rockets and remove ourselves from the highly competitive job shop business. However, he was adamant and said that he preferred to continue producing metal parts as we had been successfully doing and did not care to "reach for the moon."

As a result of our differing views on the future for Horning-Cooper, Wayne offered to sell and I reluctantly bought his interest in the company. I hated to lose Wayne as a partner, but I was determined to try building weather rockets. I changed the company name to Cooper Development Corporation and continued to work with JPL, Grand Central Rocket Company, and the U.S. Army in Huntsville, Alabama.

I restructured the management teams for CDC. I placed Orin Harvey, my friend and ex-boss at Lights, Inc., as director of administration. Beecher Williams, the former chief engineer for Lights, Inc., was appointed director of engineering. Bud Van Mannen, one of Horning's original employees, became director of manufacturing. The Cooper Development management team was ready for its new challenge of building weather rocket systems and other upper atmospheric sounding projectiles.

I had known and worked with these men for several years. We had become an experienced and capable management team, although we had little working capital, no rocket systems experience, and only marginal engineering ability. There was no one in our organization with a college degree. But still, we were determined to give it a try.

With the idea of "making do" with what we had, we put the Runt Pig Principle to work; we took a look around, and discovered that the necessary help and materials were available to us. Cal Tech and JPL had the most competent scientific and engineering talent in the world. Since we had an exceptionally good relationship with these two groups, we could turn to them for their scientific and engineering skills on a consulting basis.

Our first job from JPL was to produce the experimental metal parts for the LOKI. Once JPL had finished the development phase of the project, the Army in Huntsville ordered two hundred complete LOKI missiles. These missiles comprised an aluminum casing motor and a free-flying steel dart filled with explosives. They were designed by JPL for the Army as a weapon to shoot down high altitude aircraft.

It became apparent to us, however, that by simply modifying the free-flying dart to carry an instruments package instead of explosives, the LOKI missile could be converted into a weather research rocket. We named our new weather rocket "WASP," for Weather Atmospheric Sounding Projectile.

The WASP became the first member in our family of weather research rockets. It served the Navy's research teams in getting instant answers to important weather questions, and helped to fill the gaps in scientific knowledge about wind profiles. The WASP also performed useful research tasks for the Navy Ordnance Laboratory, the Army Redstone Arsenal, and the Signal Corps. Finally it was employed in the International Geophysical Year programs.

Visualize high goals and the means to achieve them. Reach for the moon. You will never know what you can accomplish until you try.

27.
American Rocket Society

A s the WASP became a successful weather rocket used by various weather research teams throughout the United States, I was launched into the American Rocket Society. I attended a meeting of the society in Baltimore where I met the keynote speaker of the evening, Dr. Wernher von Braun.

Von Braun was born in Wersitz, Germany, and received his Ph. D. from the University of Berlin at the remarkably young age of twenty-two. He became one of the world's leading rocket scientists. At the end of the Second World War in 1945, von Braun and his associates were brought to the United States. They were employed by the U.S. Army, and placed at Fort Bliss, Texas, near the White Sands, New Mexico, missile range.

Cooper Development Corporation had been involved with JPL in the complete development process of the LOKI missile and was selected by the Army to help Grand Central Rocket Company produce two hundred complete LOKI missiles.

Wernher von Braun took an interest in the LOKI and tendered a proposal for a "minimum satellite vehicle." This proposal included a cluster and staging of LOKI motors to power the second, third, and fourth stages. The first stage was to be one of von Braun's converted V-2 rockets, named "Redstone." Von Braun had helped the Army locate and bring a number of V-2 rockets to the United States after World War II.

Following von Braun's inspiring speech on the possibility of space exploration, I went forward to congratulate him. Much to my pleasure, he asked me to speak with him in private following the meeting.

We stepped into a bar adjacent to the meeting room and ordered a couple of imported German beers. Von Braun pulled a letter from his coat pocket and handed it to me. He said he had asked for the privilege of delivering the letter personally so that we could become acquainted. The beer arrived and we began discussing various space-related programs, including the launching of America's first satellite. Von Braun appreciated my interest in weather rockets and told me that converting the LOKI missile into a weather research rocket was an exceptional achievement, especially considering the scarcity of funds available for scientific rockets.

"Please tell me more about yourself, Clifford," he said.

I told him something about my boyhood in the Texas Dust Bowl and how I learned from my mother the important lesson of how to "make do." Von Braun enthusiastically delved into any subject that captured his attention. He was fascinated by my efforts to install vertical turbine pumps in the Texas Panhandle. Although there was nothing comparable to the Dust Bowl in Germany, he told me that he could easily relate to the problems I faced and overcame on the high plains in Texas. His father, he told me, had been a highly placed agriculture official in Germany and that he understood some of the problems involved in optimizing food production.

"I see some similarities between the vertical turbine pump business and the rocket business," I said. "By staging selected pump bowls, one can lift a payload of water from under the ground to the surface, allowing irrigation systems to turn arid land into productive farm land. Likewise, by staging and clustering selected rocket motors to lift a payload of weather instruments to a given altitude, rockets can be used to acquire data and help man understand and try to improve weather conditions."

Von Braun liked the comparison. We talked about how weather research might one day help man produce more food and reduce poverty throughout the world. Information gathered and analyzed might show scientists how to gain better control over weather conditions. Perhaps someday researchers might learn how to moderate hurricanes, cyclones, hailstorms, dust storms, and excessive rain or drought. Von Braun encouraged me to continue building weather rockets and other scientific research probes. Despite the race to reach the moon and outer space, we both agreed that there remained plenty of important problems to solve "locally" in the Earth's atmosphere.

Having spent the evening talking with von Braun, I now truly felt a part of America's rocket society. I could see the importance of just getting started. Little did I know early on that what began as a small project in Uncle Frank's $100-a-month rented garage would blossom into a successful rocket business.

Set up shop. Use your contacts. Go to work and enjoy the challenge.

28.
Project ASP

T he United States atomic tests and result-ant radioactive fallout became a major is-sue in 1955 and 1956. Winds carrying contaminated fallout moved steadily across national boundaries, and many governments were clamor-ing for an end to atmospheric testing. Adlai Stevenson and his running mate, Estes Kefauver, used this issue in their effort to defeat President Eisenhower for his second term.

The Japanese were especially vocal in their criti-cism of the U.S. testing programs, as the tests were being carried out in their backyard — Eniwetok and Bikini in the Marshall Islands.

The possibility of a test moratorium was being discussed. There arose an immediate demand that our nuclear labs endeavor to produce "clean" bombs. President Eisenhower authorized a crash program to check radioactive fallout in our current atomic test programs.

I received a call one day from Col. Lavier, who was attached to the Armed Forces Special Weapons Project (AFSWP) located in the Pentagon. Col. Lavier asked if it would be possible for me to come to Washington, D.C. immediately to discuss a critical need of the U.S. Government. I told him I would be there as soon as I could arrange transportation.

I took the "red-eye" flight that night and was processed next morning through clearance in the lower area of the Pentagon. I was ushered into a conference room where Col. Lavier and his associates were ready to present their problem. It was emphasized that what I was about to hear was not to be revealed to anyone except those who had an absolute need to know.

"Operation Red Wing," a series of atomic tests, was the subject of the discussion. Samples of atomic cloud formations had to be taken immediately after detonation. It was thought that the bombs to be tested might produce less harmful radioactive fallout, thus defusing the criticism of the U.S. atomic testing program. The officers explained that these atomic tests would be carried out in the Pacific, at Bikini and Eniwetok, within six months.

I was told that members of the president's Scientific Advisory Council had suggested the use of sounding rockets to test atomic clouds. Members of the council from Cal Tech, knowing our company and our work, had recommended that we be called as a potential contracting source. Col. Lavier informed me that larger companies had been approached to look at the problem, but that they were of the opinion that it would take at least two years to develop and test a rocket system capable of accomplishing this mission — *if* it was at all possible.

"We have only six months," Lavier emphasized. Would we be willing to make a proposal? This was a Friday afternoon. I asked the colonel to give me the weekend to think it over.

I went back to my hotel room and called my business associates, Orin Harvey and Beecher Williams, at their homes. After discussing my conference with AFSWP, they felt that we were not qualified to take on this project. We lacked the engineering talent needed to design a complicated rocket system. In fact, we did not have one graduate engineer on our payroll. Converting JPL's LOKI missile to our WASP weather rocket did not require engineering design talent.

In spite of our limiations, I was not ready to give up. We had recently employed A. B. Pittinger to help us with WASP sales. He had some skill in making rocket proposals. I asked Harvey to have Pittinger come to Washington to help me prepare a proposal in case I figured out how to meet this challenge.

I recognized that this was a great opportunity for our company. This project could help us realize our long-range goal of building a complete rocket system. If we could design and build a rocket for this project, it could be used for many additional scientific probes. The growth of CDC would be advanced significantly in a very short period of time. *If* we could do it.

Here was another chance to solve a problem and create tremendous value by applying the Runt Pig Principle to the highly technical rocket business. CDC had a proven management team and an excellent rocket manufacturing capability. The needed engineering talent could be acquired from JPL or Cal Tech on a part-time consulting basis. Also, we were experienced at subcontracting and knew the specialized businesses that produced reliable quality work.

My good friend, Chuck Bartley, president of Grand Central Rocket Company, could help us design and produce the motor. He was a former JPL employee and one of the most capable solid propellant engineers in the country. I called Chuck and he joined me in Washington, D.C. We discussed the project requirements and started assisting Pittinger in his effort to put together a proposal. It was a difficult job. How to bid on a job when we didn't even know the environmental ramifications of an exploding atomic bomb to be detonated on an island in the South Pacific? How could a reliable tracking station be established? Could we place a receiving station underground? Would it withstand the shock of an atomic blast? Given that telemetry has severe drifting problems, could we track the rockets with instruments from a ship at sea?

No rocket had yet been produced that could

achieve the desired trajectory. A new metal casing would have to be designed and built for the solid propellant rocket motor. Devising an instrument package which would sense and acquire the needed data would be a most difficult task.

After many hours of phone conference calls and with Chuck Bartley's and Pittinger's help, we put together a proposal. I called Col. Lavier on Monday and informed him that we were ready to present a proposal and that if it was acceptable, we would need a contract commitment immediately. Time, we knew, would be our greatest enemy.

Lavier called a conference of AFSWP scientific personnel to review our proposal. The attendees were all experienced with atomic testing and represented all phases of the scientific and engineering professions. Pittinger presented our proposal and I joined him to help answer the questions.

One person wanted to know something about the qualifications of our personnel. "Mr. Cooper," he asked, "how many Ph. D.'s do you have on your payroll?"

I answered, "Enough to handle the project."

Another individual demanded, "Why do you think you can do this in six months when others better qualified consider it a two-year effort?"

My reply was, "We'll put two years of human effort into this project in six months. It's not the number of days that count, but what one accomplishes during those days. We'll give this job our very best effort."

Another officer asked us how we could do the project for $750,000, when others thought it would take millions. I replied that time was money, and the more time we save the less it costs. I explained that our estimate was based on the amount of money we could intelligently and efficiently spend in six months. Fewer people on the payroll, I added, will give those assigned responsibilities the freedom and incentive to be optimally productive.

One last question concerned the financial strength and assets of CDC. My answer was a heartfelt, "My people are my greatest assets."

Apparently these were the words they wanted to hear, because after the conference, Col. Lavier informed me that they would like to let us give it a try. The price was right. We would not be penalized if we did not accomplish the mission. It was worth the money to have us do our best. If we did not get the data this time, we could try again during the next series of tests in two years.

We did not have one day to spare. To save time I suggested that the Bureau of Ships be our contracting agent, as we had just finished negotiating a simple modification contract with them and they held a complete file on CDC. I assured Col. Lavier that if he'd give us a letter of intent, we would start immediately. A letter was produced and I caught the next plane to California.

I needed a qualified, experienced engineer who could take charge of the project and give it design and production direction. John G. Small of JPL came to mind. He was familiar with our people and knew our manufacturing ability. I set up an appointment to see him the next day.

John said that he was flattered, but after hearing the scope of the project, suggested an associate at JPL, Chuck Zimney, who he felt was a better choice and would be challenged by the tough assignment. I was impressed with Chuck's qualifications and found him enthusiastic about the proposal. I agreed to let him pick two associates from JPL whom he considered best qualified to help with the project. He chose Austin G. "Tex" McLaughlin, a rocket design engineer, and Don Fite, an experienced electronics engineer.

The next day I visited JPL to discuss the project with Dr. Pickering, its director, and to get his evaluation of Zimney, McLaughlin and Fite. After hearing of the critical nature of the project, he agreed that they were qualified for the assignment, but he felt that it was not possible to accomplish the mission in six months. He suggested that I was pretty gutsy to take on the assignment under such time constraints. He wished me good luck, but at the same time, expressed reluctance to let Tex go because he would be difficult to replace. I was in no position to press him on this matter. In the meantime, Zimney had approached Tex and they made arrangements to meet at our plant that evening.

Before I arrived for our meeting, Tex had reviewed the project with Zimney. During our interview I discovered that he had been raised in the Texas Panhandle, which caused us to be very comfortable with one another. Austin G. "Tex" McLaughlin was a true product of the high plains of Texas. He had a dry sense of humor and spoke with the characteristic Panhandle twang. I asked him if he thought a rocket could be designed and produced to accomplish the proposed task. He answered, "I sure would like to see us give her a try."

There was something in the way he responded, his quiet, modest confidence that made me understand why Dr. Pickering did not want to lose him. He reminded me of my good friend and partner, Leroy Aven. Like Leroy, Tex was smart and honest, a man I felt sure I could rely on when faced with a most difficult assignment.

The next day, Dr. Pickering called to say that Tex had asked for and received permission to join CDC. I now felt confident that by adding the design team of Zimney, McLaughlin and Fite to our existing management organization of Harvey, Williams and Van Mannen we were now capable of designing and producing a complete rocket system.

Zimney was elected a director of CDC and put in charge of the project. The team worked exceptionally well together. Every employee felt challenged by his assignment and fiercely motivated to succeed. We named our project ASP for Atmospheric

Sounding Projectile. The fun had just begun.

We had to conceive, develop, test, and produce a rocket system that was capable of penetrating atomic bomb blasts at predetermined points, with instruments to relay the data by telemetry to stations underground and at sea. After the development phase had been proven, we would manufacture fifty systems. These fifty rockets and launchers would be delivered to the Pacific proving ground where a concrete underground receiving station was to be built. Another receiving station was to be set up on a ship at sea. We could not ask for one extra minute of time. The rockets must be on the launchers and ready when the bombs dropped. They would be ignited by the flash from the bombs.

We did not have time to hold regular meetings. Most decisions were made while we were walking together through the shop or during car trips to outside suppliers.

Enthusiasm for the project was contagious. Night after night I would go by the plant on my way home and find the lights on and employees still working. We tried to limit the hours they worked but were unable to do so. Hourly employees would come in the back door and "forget" to punch the time clock on weekends in order to get their job done.

Four months later, on Christmas Day, our team was at Point Mugu getting our first test firing ready to detonate. On December 27, we had a successful firing. Everything worked as anticipated. We then produced fifty ASP rockets and launchers. Zimney, Fite, McLaughlin, and Fred Saltis took them to the Pacific, had the underground and ship receiving stations set up, and installed the rockets on their launchers. All were in place when the bombs dropped.

The story was told in the Congressional Record and in letters from Admiral Mumma, our contracting officer from the Bureau of Ships. Yes, we gathered the critical data and we did it in six months, not two years. We did it for $750,000, not millions of dollars.

Our ASP rocket went on to be useful in many other tough assignments. Cooper Development Corporation became one of America's first successful rocket systems companies.

It is necessary to match, motivate, and challenge people in order to solve problems and achieve success in a collective human effort.

29.
Sixty Seconds to Catch a Sunflare

J uly 1, 1957 marked the beginning of the worldwide International Geophysical Year. This was an eighteen-month period during which sixty-two countries conducted scientific studies of the earth, the oceans, and outer space, sharing their findings. The National Academy of Sciences directed the activities of the United States in the various research projects. One of the subjects to be studied was sunflares. Dr. Herbert Friedman of the Navy Research Lab was in charge of these studies. He was familiar with our ASP and WASP rockets with their potential for weather research and called to see if Cooper Development Corporation could assist him.

The sunflare program would consist of a series of fourteen rocket firings to take place over a three-month period. After reviewing Dr. Friedman's needs, we checked to see what rocket motors were already available and capable of meeting his requirements. We proposed the use of an ASP rocket, which we could stage on top of an Army Nike missile motor. The Nike motors were in Army inventory and were available to us. We could call this combined ASP and Nike "ASPEN." We were awarded a contract to design, manufacture, field launch, and help record data from fourteen ASPEN rocket firings.

Dr. Friedman came to California with his associate, Dr. Chubb, to oversee the final days of preparation and the launching of our first ASPEN rocket. I arranged for him to speak to the Alhambra Rotary Club about the project.

He pointed out in his speech that the sun is 332,000 times larger than the earth, hundreds of millions of miles away, and a source of immeasurable energy. Sunflares, he explained, leap into space from the surface of the sun at velocities that stagger the imagination. They occur without warning, last but a few minutes, and are a matter of great scientific curiosity. Scientists believe that they dramatically affect weather on earth.

Weather has always been one of man's greatest interests, Dr. Friedman went on to explain. Since prehistoric times, men have looked to the sky for clues to better understand how weather works. The more we know about weather, the better chance we have to control and improve our living conditions on earth.

Precise timing was absolutely essential to capture sunflare information. The instruments had to be placed 150 miles up in less than three seconds in order to catch the sunflares at the moment of eruption. Since we were researching a phenomenon never before studied with rockets, much of what we did was purely experimental.

Launched at an 80° angle, the ASPEN would require only a 60-second countdown. The 12-foot Nike booster, using solid propellant fuel was to thrust the ASP to a height of 50,000 feet, at which point the ASP would ignite and carry its payload of instruments to burnout, then coast to apogee at nearly 150 miles. At that point, it would set on its tail and yaw, moving in a manner that caused the rocket to rotate on its vertical axis. This movement would allow the instruments to take a look at the sunflares and send back the data to the receiving station in our trailer.

The first ASPEN was to be detonated at Point Mugu, a few miles north of our plant in Monrovia, California. The day of the launching I picked Dr. Friedman and Dr. Chubb up at the Huntington Hotel in Pasadena and drove them to the site. In the car we had a chance to become better acquainted, and as we drove through the beautiful Oxnard farmland I discovered that both men were interested in agriculture. They were fascinated by the application of deep-well vertical turbine pumps to irrigation farming. I told them how I first saw, and was inspired by, these productive fields, an experience which later led me to transfer the same irrigation technology to my home country on the high, dry plains of Texas. We found it interesting that in this same advanced agricultural area, we would study the effects of sunflares on weather, knowing how dramatically weather affects farming.

At Point Mugu we stood by nervously anticipating the results of our first rocket launching. A split second after detonation we realized that we were standing too close. The concussion was much stronger than we had expected and I was nearly knocked off my feet. However, the launching was a complete success. During the next few weeks, all fourteen ASPEN rockets performed perfectly, allowing Dr. Friedman and Dr. Chubb to obtain their sunflare data and make a substantial contribution to weather research.

There is nothing more exciting and satisfying than working on projects that may benefit all humankind.

30.
America's First Satellite

I n 1955, President Eisenhower threw down the gauntlet when he announced that the United States would attempt to launch the first satellite to orbit the earth. The Department of Defense appointed the Stewart Committee to investigate existing rocket hardware and to solicit proposals for a satellite from the Army, the Navy, and the Air Force. Each of the services made its own presentation. By a five-to-three vote the award was given to the Navy's Vanguard proposal.

When the Soviet Union beat the U.S. by launching Sputnik I on October 4, 1957, gloom and doom spread across the nation. It seemed impossible that Americans had to resign themselves to second place. No one was more disappointed than Wernher von Braun who had presented the Army's satellite proposal to the Stewart Committee. He was convinced that if the committee had selected the proposal, the U.S. would have been first in the space race.

Under the direction of Grand Central Rocket Company, CDC was selected to produce the third-stage air frame for the Vanguard rocket. We continued other projects for the Army and JPL, and I maintained friendly working relationships with Dr. Pickering and his associates, Dr. Jack Froehlich and John Small. I also kept up my friendship with von Braun and saw him from time to time at Rocket Society meetings. On one of my trips to Huntsville, von Braun, who was naturally interested in the progress of the Vanguard, asked me how the Navy's project was coming along.

"I can't speak for the entire project," I told him, "but we're having great success with our third-stage component."

He frowned and shook his head, "Clifford, your third-stage will never get a chance to perform. As I see it, the liquid stages ahead of yours will malfunction and the rocket will melt on the launcher."

Von Braun, one of the world's foremost authorities on liquid propellants, turned out to be dead right. On December 6, 1957, just two months after Sputnik I, the first Vanguard was detonated. In less than one second after lift-off, an improper engine start caused the first stage engine to lose thrust. The vehicle settled back on the launcher stand and exploded. On February 5th, 1958, another launch was attempted. After fifty-seven seconds of normal flight, the vehicle again broke up.

President Eisenhower immediately authorized the Army to proceed with the proposal von Braun had originally presented. Now, after Sputnik's successful launch and our two dramatic failures, the United States had decided to put its highly-qualified second team into the race.

Dr. Pickering and General Medaris agreed on a tight eighty-day deadline to complete the project. They felt confident of this schedule because of the work their two organizations had already completed on the *Jupiter C* re-entry test vehicle. This vehicle could be modified to carry a satellite into orbit. It was to be named *Explorer.*

Dr. Froehlich headed up the JPL team. Also playing a major role in the project was Dr. James Van Allen of the University of Iowa. He was the first to test the captured V-2 German rockets upon their arrival at the White Sands proving grounds in New Mexico. At this time he was working with the Vanguard team. Dr. Pickering proposed that Van Allen's instrument package (which went on to discover the radiation belts around the earth) designed for the Vanguard program, be transferred to the new *Explorer* satellite.

JPL assigned Cooper Development Corporation the major manufacturing, final assembly, and testing of the three upper stages of the rocket system, including the satellite. This project required that a new explosion-proof facility be built in Rialto, some thirty miles east of our plant in Monrovia.

Seeking the simplest and most dependable hardware for the upper three stages, JPL and von Braun decided to use fifteen scaled-down Sargent motors, clustered and stacked in a pyramid configuration. Both the second and third stages were housed in a spinning tub atop the first stage. The fourth stage, which thrust the satellite into orbit, was attached to the satellite package and sat on top of the tub.

After CDC put the complete assembly through its final test, it was shipped to Cape Canaveral, Florida, and placed on top of von Braun's modified *Redstone Jupiter C.* We were now ready to save face for the United States

Each one of us who had worked so diligently on the project kept our fingers crossed, willing our first attempt to be successful. On January 31, 1958, at 7:48 a.m. Pacific Standard Time, *Explorer I* was thrust into orbit, restoring the confidence of a nation shaken by the Soviet Union's successful launch three months earlier. *Explorer 1* (a model of which is now on display at the Smithsonian Institution) helped place the United States back on a course of scientific primacy in space.

> Don't be afraid of large or complicated problems. They are only a cluster or staging of smaller, simpler problems. Find a solution to each of the small problems and the large ones will be solved.

Orin Harvey, Cliff Cooper, and A.B. Pittinger with the ASP and WASP rockets.

Bud Van Mannen, standing, inspects the final assembly of an
ASP rocket on launcher.

DEPARTMENT OF THE NAVY
BUREAU OF SHIPS
WASHINGTON 25, D. C.

IN REPLY REFER TO
QM/Cooper Development
 Corporation(115)
NObs-72000
Ser 110-2688

1 4 NOV 1956

Mr. Clifford Cooper, President
Cooper Development Corporation
2626 South Peck Road
Monrovia, California

My dear Mr. Cooper:

I note with great pleasure that Horning-Cooper Incorporated, now the Cooper Development Corporation, successfully met an unusual challenge in developing and producing within a brief time limit a new type of rocket under Contract NObs-72000 with the Bureau of Ships.

The Navy required within six months the development and production of a low cost, high performance rocket for the purpose of obtaining high altitude scientific data. To achieve this goal, it was necessary to develop a rocket larger than any previous rocket of its type, using a new type of solid-propellant rocket motor and a special instrumented head of a type never before produced.

The general reaction of the industry was that it was not possible to complete this contract in the short time specified. Nevertheless, it was decided that the previous experience of Horning-Cooper in this field made it likely that your Company could meet the deadline. The contract was awarded to your Company, but with no penalty attached for failure to complete the contract on time.

With your entire organization gearing itself to the accomplishment of this imposing task, your engineering and technical personnel succeeded in overcoming in rapid order the developmental problems involved. In addition to those mentioned above, they solved the problem of a suitable light weight motor casing for this high altitude rocket through the application of sound engineering principles. As a result of these efforts, the required production of 50 of these rockets was achieved within the six-month time limit. It should be noted that during this short time, trial rockets had to be engineered, fabricated and thoroughly field tested prior to final production.

The new rocket, called the ASP (Atmospheric Sounding Projectile), is now being used successfully for research in the upper atmosphere, which will have an important bearing on our national defense. Your Company and its personnel are to be commended for a notable contribution to this nation's constant task of maintaining its technological superiority as insurance against aggression.

Sincerely yours,

A. G. Mumma
Rear Admiral, USN
Chief of Bureau

Letter from Rear Admiral Mumma regarding the ASP project.

A group of ASP rockets ready for launching during "Operation Redwing" in the Pacific Islands, Eniwetok atoll.

Cooper Development Corporation employees stand before the ASPEN rocket which is ready to be launched at Point Mugu, California.

The ASPEN rocket, with the CDC name on the side, is fired
off during the Project Sunflare launchings, 1957.

Secretary of the Army, Wilber M. Brucker, presents an award to Cliff Cooper in recognition of CDC's contributions to the *Explorer I* project. (See close-up below.)

UNITED STATES ARMY

in recognition

OF NOTABLE CONTRIBUTIONS TO THE PROGRAM WHICH CULMINATED IN THE LAUNCHING AND ORBITING ON 31 JANUARY 1958 OF THE UNITED STATES ARMY'S EXPLORER I – AMERICA'S FIRST RESPONSE TO THE CHALLENGE OF OUTER SPACE – THIS AWARD IS PRESENTED TO

COOPER
DEVELOPMENT CORPORATION

31 JANUARY 1959
WASHINGTON D.C.

WILBER M. BRUCKER
SECRETARY OF THE ARMY

A gathering of some of the men largely responsible for launching America's first satellite. From left to right: Cliff Cooper, Dr. W.H. Pickering, Dr. Jack Froehlich, Dr. Wernher von Braun, and Dr. James A. Van Allen.

Wernher von Braun and Cliff Cooper.

John G. Small of the Jet Propulsion Laboratory with the upper stages of America's first satellite. It is ready to be shipped from Cooper Development's plant to Cape Canaveral, Florida.

Roy Marquardt, Cliff Cooper and *Explorer I*, America's first
satellite, at the Smithsonian Institution in Washington, DC.

Epilogue

T he success of Cooper Development Corporation as a rocket systems company, and its part in the launching of America's first satellite thrust me into a new world of wealth. The United States government began appropriating large sums of money to research and build space vehicles capable of carrying man to the moon and beyond to outer space. The fledgling aerospace industry became a geopolitical weapon in the Cold War.

Our small company had become a valuable component of the new industry. I was approached by various larger companies which wanted to buy or merge with CDC. Also, several investment bankers offered to take our company public in order to raise the capital needed to keep pace with an expanding, dynamic market.

But for me, the fun was over. I had spent enough time in Washington, D.C. to know that political marketing for large government programs was not what I wanted to do with my life. Furthermore, it appeared to me that in the race to spend large sums of money to build manned space vehicles, we were overshooting and overlooking some of our most fundamental problems. Our national policies and priorities were in need of review. We really needed to address ways to improve weather conditions, to learn to keep our atmosphere clean, to desalt ocean water economically, and to formulate a national fresh water distribution system, to mention a few.

As I began to examine my own priorities, I realized that I did not want to join the stampede for big, fast bucks and get lost in the financial woods in a quest for more wealth and power. I decided to accept a most attractive offer to sell my company to the Laurence Rockefeller-financed Marquardt Corporation.

I bought the visible symbol of success, a big house surrounded by oak trees and gardens, along with the necessary staff to maintain it all. I became more active in the Young Presidents Organization. Celebrating my "big fortieth" birthday, I was the self-made man with major choices to make: Beefeaters or Tanqueray; one olive or two in very dry martinis served up in chilled glasses. I took up golf and started playing almost every day at the San Gabriel Country Club... Became the gin rummy champion of the club... Started "big dogging" my friends... Thought I had arrived, but much like the earlier times in my growth, I was sick with "big shot-itis."

The Runt Pig Principle had always worked for me, but I did not enjoy living high on the hog. Fortunately, boredom soon set in and I began to see my life taking a direction I didn't like. I needed to take control. I looked for and found some new and interesting ventures which gave me the pleasure of using my strengths and abilities. I found that solving problems and creating value contribute to a happy and successful life. When all is said and done, problems keep life interesting, and solving them makes it enjoyable.

"The Principles"

The greatest solutions, like the greatest joys in life, are often the simplest ones. Look around and see what is available to you. Use your strengths. Be willing and happy to work for what you want. When given the opportunity and proper encouragement, even the tiniest runt can grow into a strong, healthy and valuable creature.

Success and happiness depend upon how well you match with your friends, your spouse, and your business partners.

When expert advice is available to you, don't be too proud to ask for it and use it.

Imagination, initiative, energy, and determination are the keys to solving problems and creating value.

Dreams fuel the world. Be bold in chasing your own.

There are no defeats, only momentary delays. It is important to keep your goals firmly in mind and to continue to pursue them.

Stand up for your beliefs. Be true to yourself, for honesty breeds confidence and self-respect — absolute necessities for a successful, happy, and creative life.

Life should be a constant quest for learning and growth. Every experience offers an opportunity to acquire knowledge.

Too much success, too fast, can lead to unrealistic expectations. A dose of realism, while unpleasant, is helpful in keeping your feet firmly placed on your chosen path.

There are no perfect products, services, or systems. Every job offers opportunities to make improvements. Be innovative and express your ideas.

It is just as important to discover what you don't want in life as it is to decide on what you do want.

"The Principles"

Growth and change are vital for a healthy, successful life, but it is important to review and retrace our steps to make sure we have chosen the right path.

Hold firm to your deeply held beliefs. You will be rewarded with self-respect and the loyalty of true friends.

Much can be said for starting at the bottom without recommendations or inside contacts. There is no better way to learn the fundamentals of a business and gain the necessary self-confidence to move on in that business or another.

Sometimes it is difficult to solve problems in a complicated bureaucratic system. A simple, direct and even blunt approach will often work, but you must first be sure of your facts.

If you believe in something and you feel committed to it, stick with it. Look around to see what resources are available to you. Analyze all the needs and your ability to satisfy them. Then go for it!

When making a deal, negotiating a trade, or establishing a business relationship, try to make arrangements that benefit all parties involved.

When the solution to a problem is important to you, be creative. Explore substitutes and alternatives. There is usually an answer to every problem.

Active participation in service organizations, such as the Jaycees and Rotary International, will give you the opportunity to develop lasting friendships. You may also have the good fortune to meet inspirational leaders.

Seek out opportunities to contribute to community, state and national affairs. Be useful and helpful to new friends. Compensation may exceed your expectations.

"The Principles"

Strive to be honest. Speak your mind, for mutual respect comes from honest and free communication. Although it is important to hold your own opinions about a person, avoid being too quick to make judgments.

Physical attractiveness is a wonderful asset. However, in order to win a crown, beauty must be balanced with good character, personality, and achievement.

Don't be captured by glittering offers. Being your own person is far more rewarding than being someone else's puppet.

Work for causes in which you truly believe. Your efforts will not only advance those causes, but will also allow you to learn and grow. You may find that doors will open to new opportunities and influential people.

There are no failures — only stumbling blocks on the road to success. Learn as much as you can from your mistakes, and move on.

Visualize high goals and the means to achieve them. Reach for the moon. You will never know what you can accomplish until you try.

Set up shop. Use your contacts. Go to work and enjoy the challenge.

It is necessary to match, motivate, and challenge people in order to solve problems and achieve success in a collective human effort.

There is nothing more exciting and satisfying than working on projects that may benefit all humankind.

Don't be afraid of large or complicated problems. They're only a cluster or staging of smaller, simpler problems. Find a solution to each of the small problems and the large ones will be solved.

ORDER FORM

To order additional copies of *The Runt Pig Principle*, please complete the following order form and return it along with your check or money order payable to:

Alliance For Progress Publishers
P. O. Box 5581
Balboa Island, California 92662

Questions? Please call:
(714) 675-8438

Name _____

Street Address _____

City _____

State _____   Zip Code _____

Telephone   (____)   _____ - _____

	Quantity	Total
The Runt Pig Principle, $12.95 each:	_____	$ _____
California Residents Add Applicable Tax:		$ _____
Shipping & Handling:		$ _____

Book rate: $1.95 for the first book;
85¢ for each additional book

TOTAL PAYMENT ENCLOSED: $ _____

You may return any books purchased from us for a full refund,
for any reason, no questions asked.

(Please allow four to six weeks for delivery.)